A Funny Thing
Happened on
the Way

By the same author

Why I'm Not a Millionaire

A Funny Thing Happened on the Way

Nancy Spain

WEIDENFELD & NICOLSON

First published in Great Britain in 1964 by
Hutchinson & Co (Publishers) Ltd
This paperback edition published in 2021 by Weidenfeld & Nicolson
an imprint of The Orion Publishing Group Ltd
Carmelite House, 50 Victoria Embankment
London EC4Y 0DZ

An Hachette UK Company

10 9 8 7 6 5 4 3 2 1

A CIP catalogue record for this book is
available from the British Library.

ISBN (Mass Market Paperback) 978 1 4746 1865 6
ISBN (eBook) 978 1 4746 1866 3
ISBN (Audio) 978 1 4746 1867 0

Typeset by Input Data Services Ltd, Somerset
Printed in Great Britain by Clays Ltd, Elcograf S.p.A.

www.orionbooks.co.uk
www.weidenfeldandnicolson.co.uk

Foreword to the Original Edition

Always unpredictable, Nancy rang up to say she could not come to the office after all with the final, revised script of *A Funny Thing* . . . She was off on a story, but would we please collect it from Jonnie's office (Joan Werner Laurie, with whom she shared a house, features prominently in this book).

We collected the script, and I took it home to read over the weekend, the weekend of the Grand National. It was open on my desk on that Saturday when the unbelievable news was announced. A plane had crashed. Five were dead, among them Nancy and Jonnie.

Although this book was finished only a few days before she died, it had been a long time in the writing. Nancy wanted her books to have the spontaneous freshness of one of her live television programmes, but much art and hard work was needed to produce this extempore effect. There had been several drafts of this one before she was satisfied.

If, in the circumstances, the title seems inappropriate to some people, it should be said that this was the title she had chosen and we did not think it should be altered.

In my opinion her best book, this is certainly a good

one to remember her by. She was first and foremost and triumphantly an entertainer. She loved to make people laugh. She wanted people to share her enjoyment of life. That is the way we remember her, and that is the essence of these pages.

Contents

Most areas in the world may be placed in latitude and longitude, described chemically in their earth, sky and water . . . Then there are others where fable, myth, preconception, love, longing, or prejudice step in and so distort a cool, clear appraisal that a kind of high-coloured magical confusion takes permanent hold. Greece is such an area.

– JOHN STEINBECK: *Travels with Charley*

For the Middle-Aged 1963

    Good. There's a pang of passion in my heart
Confusing and surprising me. Something
    Of how I lost my ignorance. And art
Acquired taught me the way to swim. Remembering
    Old joys that grown-ups hold in cool derision.
Faith in myself. Belief in human good –
    Youth. Childhood. If you like: ambition.

    Where did I lose it? Somewhere on the way
In the gay gritty gutter of the world, The Street,
    Where nine-day wonders only last a day
Before they sink un-noticed in the Fleet?
    Yes, I ran grinning then because I knew so much
(Unprintable of course) which News Boys shout,
    Rustproof and galvanised because in touch
With all the lads whose lust is finding out.

    Ambition lost but innocence intact,
Here I am, battered to my bleeding knees
    Feeling eighteen but forty-six in fact
Finding I still react to every breeze.
    Finding in spite of all I know that I still *care,*
That after all these years I've no defence,
    Proving that life is something we can share,
Our only sin a bored indifference.

N.B.S.

BOOK ONE

To the Island, with Love

Prologue

My doorbell finally rang. I had been in a tremendous fidget waiting for it to do so. I was expecting Karsh, the great photographer of Ottawa, to come and take my picture.

Now, I have the sort of features that are, as they say, 'full of character' and hair that leads a life of its own. So I wondered what the man who had photographed Churchill, Sibelius, Schweitzer, Einstein for posterity, who was self-confessedly 'in search of greatness', could possibly make of *me*.

Karsh was late. Late, gentle, dark-eyed, wearing a navy-blue overcoat and a splendidly dashing hat pulled into a becoming slouch over one eye. His nose was big. His skin sallow. His handshake pliable. He kissed my hand. He murmured, 'My Dear Lady.' I felt inclined to giggle.

There was an assistant with him called Frank. Frank was huge, wearing an Artillery tie. Frank was the sort of man who is instantly in shirt-sleeves. Frank took all the furniture out of the drawing-room. He piled some of it in the garden, the remainder in the passage. Soon it was impossible to move in the house, either upstairs or down, except by clambering over a big armchair which Frank had pushed halfway into the downstairs lavatory. Then Frank put up studio lights, many of them. The lights stood, shakily, on music-stand feet. Frank attached them to a converter. The converter gave out a low and deadly humming, like something in a science-fiction film.

'Should it hum like that?' asked Karsh. 'I don't like it, that humming. Are you sure this system isn't D.C.?'

'Oh no,' said Frank, grinning. 'All the lights would have fused if that had been so . . .'

Charming, I thought, charming.

The pair of them now pulled a wooden chest into the middle of the room and piled upon it a little blue chair. They put the chair on the bath-mat so that it shouldn't slip. They pulled all the curtains to exclude the daylight. They hung long screens that suddenly changed the room into a Japanese parlour. Then they asked me to sit on top of the whole thing. I was very nervous.

Facing me now was a huge plate camera with Karsh skipping about beside it. When it first emerged from its trunk it had been broken. Karsh and Frank had then mended it, patiently. The performance so far had taken about three hours. Then it was necessary for Karsh to synchronise the flash with the camera shutter. This went on for another half an hour while I sat grimly on my little seat.

'Dear lady,' said Karsh, finally, rather as if it were my fault that the flash wouldn't synchronise, 'please leave the room.'

I left the room, climbing over a large pile of furniture to do so. Half an hour later I was called in again. Click went the shutter. Flash went the flash. But *not* together.

'Oh dear,' said Karsh.

'O thou gracious Apollo,' I said, somewhat loudly and somewhat stagily. 'Be so kind as to bestow your precious gifts of reason and sanity upon this man Karsh's apparatus here below. I have a solid silver drachma of the first century and I shall dedicate it to you, if *only* you will allow the flash to synchronise with the shutter for the next hour or so . . .'

By now, of course, the converter was 'warmed up' and everything went right. Karsh was fascinated, however, at my sudden invocation.

Later I took him to lunch at the Caprice, where we ate a roast suckling pig, drank a superb ('No, it is *noble*,' murmured Karsh) Château Margaux and became fast friends. Eventually, of course, Karsh asked to see the drachma I had dedicated to Apollo. So I produced it. It is a most satisfactory thick piece of silver. And, of course, extremely valuable, because it now belongs to Apollo.

'Don't you think that I should look after it much better for Apollo?' asked Karsh, as he hefted it gently up and down in his tiny gentle hands. An unusual thing. He had Y.K. embroidered on his *cuff*: the 'Y' for Youssef.

I hastily put the drachma away.

'No, no,' I said. 'If anything, it will be built in over the door of my little house in Greece. My house on the Greek island.'

Karsh's huge, dark, liquid eyes opened very wide.

'You have a *house*?' he repeated. 'A house? On a Greek island? How did this happen?' He laid down his knife and fork.

Slowly, idiotically, feeling here and there a little bit foolish, I began to explain.

'I went out to dinner with my doctor. Dr Newman,' I began. 'And there was a lady there, a very nice woman, and, well, she said she would go to Greece and buy us all land. And I said "Good" . . . So she did.'

'How much did it cost?' asked Karsh, taking a deep swallow of wine.

'One hundred pounds,' I said. 'To begin with . . . that is.'

'You mean you hadn't even seen it?' he asked.

'Well, I've seen it *now*,' I replied.

'No, but *then*,' Karsh insisted.

'Well, no,' I had to admit. 'I hadn't seen it. But I liked the idea.'

'So do I like the idea,' said Karsh. 'Tell me more. How much did it cost you in the end? More than one hundred pounds, I bet?'

I nodded, dumbly.

'Much, much more,' I said. And feeling slightly less

foolish, but not much, sitting there in the Caprice, I started to tell him.

SPAIN MEETS SKIATHOS

The island is quite green as Greek islands go – and the woman who sold me the land swore that the green showed there was water there. People to whom one described it would first show a gleam of envy in their eyes. Then a mask of resignation would slip across their faces. The resignation mask didn't say, 'Greek islands are not for the likes of me.' It said: 'Nancy is mad. Obviously it's a barren rock. All the Greeks are thieves. The land is always heavily mortgaged. You can't trust the peasants. In the end they will say it belongs to the Government. She'll lose a fortune, digging wells where there's no water. Even if she builds a house the Greek Government will take it away from her. And quite right too . . .'

Most of my friends were too kind to say any of this. It was just that I got used to the flat mask of unspoken thoughts. And behind the mask their unspoken thoughts seemed like a shout in my ears.

Skiathos is the name of the island. It is the most northerly of a group of islands called the Sporades, and it is the first island out, so to speak, from a big town called Bollos or Vollos, according to whether you are looking at a Greek map or an English one.

It takes about four hours to get to Skiathos from Vollos, in a regular boat, which runs every other day I

7

think. I'm not sure about this, because I've never taken it. All my visits to the island have been by caique, that is to say a broad-beamed Greek fishing boat, which picked me up (a) at a place called Pifki and (b) at a place called Orei. Orei and Pifki are about seventy miles north of Athens.

You can't load a motor-car on to a caique at Pifki because the beach there is so shallow that the caiques themselves stay far out, lolloping at anchor, while we row to them through the small, crisp, silver-blue waves in dinghies. At Orei there is a proper jetty, built of real stone: and the crew of the caique put down a couple of planks and I simply drive on slowly and carefully.

The whole operation is most matter of fact. Nobody screams or becomes hysterical. If the water was rough nobody would bother with it and the caique wouldn't sail. So long as they weren't messed about by third and intervening parties I always found the Greeks very calm and dignified, and they certainly don't steal any worse than the Neapolitans.

Skiathos itself looms out of the sea after two and a half hours' chugging from Pifki, four hours' chugging from Orei.

It is green from end to end. Green with pine trees, scrub, maquis, gorse bushes in and out of bloom, fig trees, lemon trees, even baby oak trees.

At the south-eastern tip, in the most sheltered part of the island, there is a tiny town (also called Skiathos), which from the distance on the horizon looks like white lace. Nearer, it is possible to see that the water-front actually consists of two or three restaurants (you go into the kitchen and choose what you want, you drink either retsina or local wine *without* resin in), a pharmacy, a petrol station, a church or two, some pink houses, a ship-chandler's and a village store. Behind the water-front there are paved streets made of good, dressed stone with a central drain (that presumably pours melted snow in the winter), houses, paved yards and gardens, two small hotels that look just like ordinary houses with hard clean beds and one rather gritty communal shower, and eight bakers' shops that bake grey flinty bread. There are also butchers, candlestick makers and a Calor Gas depot, as most people cook on Calor Gas.

There is electricity in the village, but the authority turns it off at midnight – just when one needs it most.

There is one road through Skiathos; rough, dusty, red earth that could when wet be clay from tip to tip. The Army are building it, and very helpful and lovely they are too.

If I shut my eyes now I can see Skiathos clearly: the bluest, greenest dream I ever saw. The blue – first the sky, then the water. The water – clear, deep and amazing. In the shallows it is green, crimping and curling over sand that shimmers like gold-dust, sand that is so hot in the summer that it burns your feet. Farther out, should you swim to the rocks, the depths turn purple far down: purple and dark blue. There are seldom cloud shadows. Occasionally a cool wind comes from the land from the north, which makes the water cold for a day or two; and then in the tail of the wind there are thin white clouds like a woman's scarf. Otherwise the sun soaks down, day after day, a sun so hot that it seems white.

The island is quite young, as islands go: about two million years old. But somehow, even when I am just thinking about it before I go to sleep, I have the impression that it has always been waiting: the last (or the first) of a long series of dream islands belonging especially to me.

Chapter One

The Island Habit

I got the island habit when I was a child, growing up in my parents' house in Newcastle upon Tyne. Before my father died, there were in a bookcase, in a room we could never learn to call anything but the nursery, two solid shelves full of island books.

Treasure Island, of course, and *The Coral Island* by Ballantyne, and *Masterman Ready* and *Robinson Crusoe*. But there was also a shelf filled with obscurer works: *White Shadows in the South Seas*, *Atolls in the Sun*, even a trashy romance called *Isle of Desire*. *Isle of Desire* was super. It was all about a young clean-limbed Englishman called Ronnie, who did not have his 'way' with his girlfriend for pages and pages while he invoked the island spirits and hunted for buried treasure. 'It wouldn't be playing the game,' cried Ronnie, passing a hand through his crisp yellow hair. Not playing the game, that is, until one full moon, when everything went too far and Ronnie and his young lady decided they were already 'married in the sight of heaven'.

Outside the nursery, beyond the life conjured up by

the island books, there was Newcastle upon Tyne. A fine city.

'A capital city without a doubt,' Ginette Spanier once said to me, adding under her breath, 'But heaven knows where it is the capital *of* . . .'

But there were an awful lot of grey streets, red bricks (a peculiarly unattractive red, too), slush in winter, rain and wind in summer. And aside from the angels' wings of the South African war memorial in the Haymarket, splurging up against a blue and white sky, nothing in the city that could be classified as 'beauty'.

Yet there was an island in the city, in the middle of the Bull Park Lake. And one birthday I was given a steam-driven 'speed boat' called *Miss America*, and I insisted, along with my cousin Taprell (Tapoo) Dorling, whose birthday was a few days later, on floating the thing, under its own steam, in the Bull Park Lake. Making a hideous clatter, *Miss America* flew off into the distance and crashed into the island. Here a sheer hulk, she drifted, against rain and wind and miniature hurricane. It took hours and hours of patient stone-throwing before we got her back, and then went, wet through and exhausted, to the cinema to see a silent movie (they didn't talk in those days) called *Second to None*. It was about the Navy in World War I. Ever after, in the family, a wet day was either 'as wet as Tapoo's birthday' or 'nearly as wet as Tapoo's birthday'. But even that island in the Bull Park Lake, tiny and dim and probably thick with duck dirt, was to me a shape of romance.

Time passed and I grew inward. I was supremely happy, of course, growing inward, and the life I led inside my own mind seemed to me immeasurably superior to that extroverted existence provided for me by my kind mother and father and, later, by my kind school-teachers.

In my mind's eye it was seldom 'nowadays'. Usually I was a charioteer, 400 years B.C., forearms ringed with heavy gold bracelets, horses straining and sweating as I held them with ingenious wrists, supple yet hard as steel. This daydream I evolved for myself when my sister told me the story of *Ben-Hur*. Again, the silent version. Or else I was a powder monkey in the *Victory* at Trafalgar. Or occasionally I would bark harsh orders to the crew of a quinquereme, coming from Nineveh and going to the isthmus. And at the back of every picture there was a blue, blue sky and a sea where the shadows were purple and the shallows silver, green and gold.

How I ever managed to attend school with my mind all full of seascape I'll never know. Or after school, when World War II should have claimed my full attention. And after that again when I became a writer . . .

I went to, anyway, three other schools besides that strictly anonymous exclusive dump in Sussex. When I was about six I also remember attending for a day or so (to keep me out of mischief) the village school in the valley of the North Tyne at a place called Tarset. I sat next door to a boy called Watty, whose shaven head was so fair that it looked white; and, mouth open, I heard him recite in a passionate Northumbrian accent

'The Spider and the Fly', 'Which way does the wind blow, which way does it blow?' and 'Three fairies came in heliotrope and one in violet', three poems that I have never heard before or since.

We used to go for our summer holidays to Tarset, where we stayed in a square grey house called Greystead Rectory or an even blanker-looking place: the Moorcock Inn. The Moorcock had a hen-run at the back, straggly pine trees and a box of well-displayed medals (including the Military Cross with its white and purple ribbon) which had been won by Mr Forster, the proprietor.

The Moorcock Inn smelt divinely of well-scrubbed floors and yesterday's beer – and in the evening, after my sister and I had gone to bed, the noise and laughter of the locals drinking and talking would rise through the white-painted ceiling to tantalise us. Outside the North Tyne sparkled, hurtled and flung itself to join the other Tyne, the South Tyne, in a series of dark brown pools, flashing shallows and (when the river 'came down deep') a smooth roaring, angry yellow sweep of water, arched in the middle as high as any of the suspension bridges along the river, leaving driftwood in the low branches of the aspens and little tufts of sheep's wool, too. Flood water often covered the road above the rectory, at a place called the Crags. This was, I imagine, the wildest most primitive countryside anyone might encounter in England in the twentieth century. There was a spring, red with iron, bubbling up in spurts like the heart-beats of a giant by the roadside. The pool into which the water

gushed was fringed with wild peppermint and fronds
of baby green bracken, curling like feathers on ladies'
hats. It was so obviously an enchanted place that even
Watty knew about it, and all the village children used
to go there for their wishes. 'It is a well belonging to
the ancient people, the old gods, the fairies,' Watty said.
What could they have wished for? I never asked them.
But years later, when I was in the throes of a love affair
more passionate than wise, I tugged my true love out to
the heather and purified us both in this wishing well . . .
and so, after a fashion, lived happy ever after. So I have
always thought of it as Apollo's spring. Everyone knows
that he loves such places.

There was no need of an inner life in the North Tyne
valley . . . anyway for me. What went on all around
me, the swallows flying low in and out of the barns,
skimming the surface of the water – the cows standing
knee-deep in the shallows, switching with their tails in
the rare but nevertheless achingly hot August drought
– the heat-shimmer above the crags, the adders pouring
away into the warm stones by the roadside – all this was
life enough. There was no need of escape from such a
place. Even the skin of a grass snake, lying shed, like
some jewel rejected by Fabergé: all these things proved
that for one month in the year at least I was not a city
child.

I was ecstatically happy up the North Tyne. But I am
not too sure that my mother and sister enjoyed it as I
did. Mother once read all the newspapers with which

Mrs Forster had lined the chest of drawers, on a day as 'wet as Tapoo's birthday', and I know my sister asked for people of her own age to play with. Since then she has reminded me that she sketched in pastels, romantically. There was a distinct lack of realism in my attitude towards that river valley.

In fact, I believe there was company – the Thompsons of the Sneep, Diana and Lydia. I suppose the Sneep to have been the name of their house or farm. With them we once went swimming in a huge deep, dark brown pool called the Wynd Burn Lynn, and Lydia knocked me down and said I must have a weak heart because my face was red. I suppose I was a cocky child and got on her nerves. So I didn't wish for company. I made up awful poems in which I was a harpist, who played for ancient chieftains in an ancient cave and held them spellbound with my magic.

When we went back to Newcastle upon Tyne, it seems, I took my mother on one side and asked to be sent to school – 'I can't be hanging around with you always' was what I (charmingly) remarked – and to school I duly went, in a white panama hat with a purple and white hat-band upon it – to Miss Thompson's of Windsor Terrace. (No relation whatsoever to the Thompsons of the Sneep.)

School at Miss Thompson's was taught by chanting. When the French mistress came in the room we all rose to our feet and chanted rhythmically, 'Bon jour, madame, com-montallyvooze-matin?' and the French mistress appropriately replied. Geography was splendid, consisting of long lists of capes and bays of England. But religious knowledge surpassed everything, when taking our time from Miss Thompson (wittily known as Tommy), we would shout:

> 'GENESIS Exodus Levit-i-cus NUMBERS
> Deuteronomy Joshua Judges RUTH . . .'

Some months ago I broadcast this memory of mine in a programme about education, and a flood of letters, mainly from ladies in their late sixties or early eighties, arrived to thank me for the broadcast and to say that they were certain that this early chanting, which they too had shared as an experience, had strengthened *their* memories. And presumably mine, too.

It's quite true that up to the age of about forty I have almost total recall, not necessarily something (let me tell you) upon which to congratulate oneself. For example, along with learning the books of the Bible, at Tommy's, I once flung a little boy called Ian into the fire simply because he was wearing a kilt and I was jealous of him. I could well do without such shaming recollections.

After I left all my schools, however, and became a journalist, I could not bear to learn shorthand. So I trained my memory to hold for me (for about twelve hours) what I wanted. If I drink too much I remember nothing at all: almost a blessing in a way, but very difficult when conducting a lengthy interview with a heavy-drinking tycoon or film star.

Why did I leave Miss Thompson's? I don't recall, so it is obviously something I don't *want* to remember. I can remember shouting out in class that dried lava was pumice stone and 'going to the top'. In this lovely old-fashioned ritual, if you answered a question right you left your lowly place and 'went up top', a highly satisfactory thing. So it may well be that having achieved greatness I did not want to go back the next day, and through *not* knowing, say, that Acropolis means 'Outside the city' lose my new-found honour.

Anyway, the next school I went to was Runton Hill, West Runton, Norfolk. It lies in between Sheringham and Cromer on the coast of Norfolk – a county which, as all the world knows, claims for itself more ancient origins and civilisation even than Northumberland. To say nothing of Sandringham and the Royal Family.

To get to West Runton from Newcastle upon Tyne was a lifetime's achievement in itself. It *could* be done by changing at Grantham and then at King's Lynn . . . but most people went to London and got a train to Norwich and *then* changed, arriving tired and cross and sleepy, with huge cinders in the eyes from peering out at the engine, worming its way through Norfolk . . .

I made a small, short-lived and somewhat futile effort at realism at Runton Hill. For example, I remember the school was divided into three houses – North, South and Bryntirion. Bryn, as it was called, was 'a villa residence

18

set in own grounds' of about one half-acre, about a mile from the other two houses. Bryn was under the rule of a dashing widow called Mrs Lipscombe, known to us as Mrs Lip. Mrs Lip dressed rather well, and always used to fling her scarf round her neck like someone at university. She wore fringed brogues that flapped, carried a walking stick when she walked and I am pretty sure she disliked us children intensely. She had good cause. We were all pretty horrible.

Frances Sherwood and I shared a room that looked down on to the half-acre. The room was called Blue. (It had blue curtains. How did you guess?) Frances was younger than I was (she was only nine), but she had the distinction of being the niece of James Elroy Flecker, the poet. Just as I grew up cringing from the great names of Mrs Beeton and Samuel Smiles (who are in *my* pedigree), so Frances's lip would curl with scorn whenever 'Uncle Roy' cropped up. 'Oh hell,' she would say, and other unmaidenly and un-nine-year-old oaths would stream from her lips. 'Why should I have to learn this stuff, simply because I'm related to the man? . . .' 'The Dying Patriot' (known to Frances as The Dying Parrot), 'Old Ships', An 'Isle', a 'Sickle Moon', the whole of 'Hassan', including Yasmin's Song, made Frances sick to her stomach and she would turn away groaning with boredom if anyone else recited them in class. I know what happened to Frances, I heard from her the other day. She is now married, lives in Australia, has three children.

Next door to Frances and myself was a rather grander

dormitory called Pink. (It had p . . . how did you?) In this room lurked, with a good deal of self-appointed leadership, Sally Shorrock, Pamela Schiele and Viola Tunnard. Sally was the head of Bryn. Her word was law. She ruled with a series of kicks, cuffs and blows. Pamela Schiele was the headmistress's niece, so I don't suppose she got kicked much. Viola was the Musician. Viola was as smart as paint. She knew when anyone was singing out of tune (it was usually me). She could play for hymn-singing rather better than Mrs Lip, who otherwise did it. Viola had a fine Byronic profile and a lock of hair worn in one real tortoiseshell hair-slide which she tossed back as she thundered away in the bass through 'Hills of the North Rejoice'. Viola has now grown up to be Joyce Grenfell's favourite accompanist, and (together with Valerie Trimble) she is often to be seen playing the piano in the background on television. In those days I was very much in awe of her. Who wouldn't be, all that sight-reading and ability to transpose keys and knowledge of harmony when the rest of us were just stumbling through Schubert's 'Marche Militaire'? I know what became of Frances and Viola, but I often wonder what became of Sally Shorrock and Pamela Schiele and the rest.

Why, because of her musical ability Viola was even singled out to be in the school play, which was performed in a part of the grounds, all low bushes and grassy mounds and pine trees, a natural if baby amphitheatre, known as the Dell. (A Mrs Fisher Prout used to conduct art classes here once a week and it was an acknowledged beauty

spot.) The play was *As You Like It* and Viola was one of
the pages who whip in, when the scene is supposed to be
changing, to sing 'It was a Lover and his Lass'. Even at
the age of eleven, when we acted out the classics, Viola
was always in the lead. I now know why. Viola was a
realist. And concentrated. The rest of us were hopeless
romantics, who were so hopelessly unconcentrated that
we didn't even know when we were singing off key.
Viola knew where Greece was on the map. She probably
knew where the Ural Mountains were. It was no good
keeping up with Viola. Before long I was daydreaming
again at Runton Hill, babyishly living inward.

At some point during my time at Runton, Miss
Harcourt, the headmistress, told me I was 'an Athenian,
a typical Athenian'. She said the words with loathing
and contempt, but I was thrilled. I went around seeing
myself in a white tunic and those gold arm-clasps, arguing with Socrates and meeting Theseus (Runton was
great on the ancient myths and legends and we acted
them out with the English mistress, who also taught gym
and needlework), until I discovered, via my mother, that
Miss Harcourt meant that I was simply 'led astray by any
new thing'.

I wonder if Viola Tunnard ever daydreamed, or was
led astray by any new thing? I bet she didn't, wasn't. Certainly she was an exceptionally clever child. She bossed
us all around. She had a knack, which can often be found
in people of strong character and personality, of making
anything (however trivial) that happened to her seem

important. For example, she won, and embroidered on her tunic, an orange triangle for gymnastics. (This was how honours and awards came to one at Runton Hill. Next one acquired an orange circle for deportment, a grey triangle going the other way for something else and a blue circle around everything else for the first lacrosse XII). We all fingered it. We all envied her. It seemed, at the very least, like laurel leaves at the Olympic Games.

But when, within a term, the rest of us, Frances (Flecker's niece) included, had acquired orange triangles – lo and behold they meant nothing, nothing at all. The virtue went out of orange triangles when they belonged to *us*.

At this school we worshipped, along with all the rest of the local parson's parishioners, at a church (rather low C. of E., I think) at Sheringham. Quite aside from the difficulty, at the age of ten or nine-and-a-half, of sitting still and listening to someone reading aloud, I have to put on record that Frances and I were secretly bound up in a cult where *we* followed (on the sly, because we were afraid that Viola would find out) Apollo. We sacrificed to him regularly in the shrubbery at the bottom of the half-acre at Bryntirion (it was turned into a tennis court with a very short run-back in the summer) and people were always asking what our little fires were *for* . . . Later in the year, when it was November and tremendous winds and frosts tore across our landscape, and Apollo had obviously hidden his face from us for ever, and the Plough and Orion seemed to spin in points of frost above us, we went in for a strong Panic urge, with frenzies and invocations and everything.

This year when I had my letter from Frances, from Australia, it enclosed an ancient rough notebook of mine, covered with drawings of Greek gods and heroes, with some pretty astonishing verses, obviously written by the ten-year-old N. Spain:

'When Glory, Lord and Honour, is all the people cry', it began, I remember, and was a more than embarrassing hymn to Apollo. It startled me that Frances should have kept it for all these years.

Our Sunday walk, after we had endured the sermon in mute and wriggling protest, was usually through a part of the Runton hinterland called the Roman Camp. Here huge toadstools (red, with big white spots) grew. Obviously the food of the gods, Frances and I thought, although we never lost ourselves so much in our cult as to pick them and eat them. (Ivy, the maid at Bryntirion, would have sneaked to Mrs Lip.) Here were wonderful thickets of sacred oak and ash and thorn, all turned golden and red by autumn frosts, and here, with the greatest of ease (if only she had stood still long enough), we could have sacrificed Pamela Schiele, the headmistress's niece.

At half-term those children who were not called for, and aggressively taken out by their parents, used to play a tremendous game up at the Roman Camp called valley netball.

Miss Vernon Harcourt, Pamela Schiele's aunt, the headmistress, had invented it. It was a very dangerous game indeed, and it too had about it all the trappings of an ancient ritual.

We used a round ball. The entire school would turn out, and stand shoulder to shoulder in two lines, like a crocodile. North would be against South, and the junior girls from Bryn would be shared out between the houses. I was usually, shamefully, picked last because I was small and light. The object of the game was for one house to touch down the ball in the opposing house's camp on the top of the opposite hillside, having crossed the valley. For a long while to be picked first in such games was my sole ambition.

Miss Vernon Harcourt would hurl the ball into the air and the game would be on. The game raged down and up the steepest valley that J.V.H. (this was her nickname, because her given name was 'Janet') could find in the Roman Camp. One might run with the ball, but when tackled one had to pass, but backwards, as in rugby football.

I used to spend most of the game face downwards in the bracken, all breath knocked from my body, while the two teams, North *and* South, tramped heavily by on my shoulder blades. But I was fairly well off. Frances sprained an ankle. Viola had long scratches down her face. Even J.V.H., bounding high in the air, tooting on her whistle, occasionally hurt herself. I imagine that for the rest of the girls of Runton Hill, valley netball has a great nostalgic significance – like the Eton Wall Game. For me it was one long, whimpering day of terror. And

I'm not all that easily scared. Turning ankles, scratched faces, bruised torsos. That was the very least of it. There was also the fact that others might know I was afraid. And there was the shaming thing of being so small and light. No wonder my mind turned inwards, to more romantic dreams.

Eventually I left Runton Hill. I'd been there long enough to win my orange triangle and develop one of those heavy chest colds which were usually a secure, safe escape from the rigours of valley netball or geography with Miss Harcourt.

It was while I was in bed with my heavy chest cold that one of the staff brought me the book *1,000 Beautiful Things*.

I lay in bed, wheezing away, inhaling Friar's Balsam, and cosily turning the pages of this splendid compilation. Wherever Arthur Mee, who edited this book, is now, I'd like to thank him. Amongst plates showing Van Dycks, Rubens, Whistler's mother, pages giving famous fragments of words: 'Three Things that Come Not Back, The Spent Arrow, the Spoken Word, the Broken Promise', I discovered the Charioteer (I still had not seen a map of Greece).

O, sweet Charioteer of Delphi, with your head the size of a pin, your face of charmed stupidity, your huge limpid agate eyes fringed with eyelashes like a doll, your glorious green bronze arm and touchingly defenceless feet, the exquisitely simple folds of your tunic, I fell in love with you that day, wheezing through the Friar's

Balsam. 'In love' is for the romantic. 'Love' for the realist.

I swore, lying there in that hard school bed, with the towel over my head and the book propped open in front of me, that one day I would 'see you plain', go to Delphi, dedicate myself to reason at the great shrine of Apollo, consult the oracle. Eventually, of course, I reached Delphi. I was frightened then, at the truth. I was so afraid that my Charioteer wouldn't be as beautiful as he was in Arthur Mee's book.

No one seems to know who the Charioteer actually was. I can't see that this matters. It is enough that he is there, as Everest is there, as Shakespeare's plays are there, as the purifying springs are there: one in the North Tyne valley, the other in the flank of Mount Parnassus, dedicated to mysteries far older than the Christ.

When I arrived at Delphi my devotion to the Charioteer was so obvious to the custodians of the museum, and evidently so pleasing to them, that they used to let me sit and stare at him for nothing, letting me in free to memorise each fold, each vein, each bone in hand and foot. Infinitely moving, I found, walking cautiously around him, were the nuts and bolts cunningly holding him together inside, keeping him upright on his plinth.

'Fear the Greeks when they bring gifts.' Somebody taught me this at one or other of my schools: and this is the first and only Greek gift I ever had, excepting the sky and the sun and the wind and the cricket noise in the silent green shade of the olive trees. I imagined those. Sitting there in bed, knees hunched to support the china jug, with the hot, sweaty towel over my head, I escaped into a world of my own with that Charioteer.

Who can say if such a romantic development of the imagination is right or wrong? I only want to put on record that it was infinitely more amusing than the hymn-singing to Viola's accompaniment downstairs in the parlour of Bryntirion, or the dreadful little dirty squares of flannel upon which we were supposed to practise cross-stitch, hemming, French knots and cable-stitch. And it was better than the slightly patronising tones of Mrs Lipscombe reading aloud to us after lunch from *The Prisoner of Zenda* or *Under the Red Robe*. Mrs Lipscombe's taste was odd, to say the least of it. She would cheerfully read an un-named romance in which the hero was sold into slavery in the Deep South and nevertheless won his Southern Belle, because of his feats of horsemanship, but she balked at Siegfried Sassoon. One term I handed her *Memoirs of a Foxhunting Man* and implored her to read aloud from that instead of all that other rubbish. (I dare say I said 'rubbish', too.) She laid the book down and remarked coldly:

'Well, I see that there is a sequel to this called *Memoirs of an Infantry Officer*. Perhaps he will amount to something in that.'

Poor Mrs Lipscombe. You're dead long ago, and your head, tossed so contemptuously over Sassoon and with such joy over Anthony Hope, is laid to rest somewhere. But that day when something angry flashed between us you paid me the compliment of treating me, nine years old and as light as a minnow, as an equal. And how you must have loathed me when you took up golf. And I patronisingly asked you what your handicap was. And you replied you had no handicap as yet. And I said, pityingly, insultingly, 'Oh, I see.'

For though I was not a realist when I was nine, for some terrible reason I have always been a realist about golf.

ON THE ROAD TO MANDA . . . WHERE?

At any time of life I would have been glad to take the offer of an escape in the idea of a Greek island of my own. But at the age of nine, ten or eleven my only allowed escape lay in reading.

The world of books: romantic, idle, shiftless world, so beautiful, so cheap compared with living. If you do not share this world how can I explain it? I have been in contact with books all my life, lately as a commodity to be bought and sold. Not since my teens have I thought of books as literature. I love books. I love the feel of them, the smell of them. I like a new clean book, freshly bound, particularly when I am the first to read it. I like dirty books – where other people have been before me, slipping fried eggs between the pages as markers – rather less.

If I dared scribble in a book as a child I was beaten. My father would take his evening slippers (they had bows on) and he would lam them into us for spoiling a book. So all my children's books are spotless. *The Wind in the Willows*, *Huckleberry Finn*: they have been read and re-read and tre-read (I only really love a book when I have read it at least four times) and are still as clean as the day they slid from the binder's hands.

My father was the literary influence in our life. He had a lyric quality, in his enthusiasms, in his dismay, that was infinitely touching. He read *Huck Finn* aloud, glorying in the flight down the Mississippi. But Kipling was my father's literary god. He admired the short stories (and the verse) extravagantly and the unending shelves of Kipling short stories in their meaningless titles, equally meaningless fine 'collected edition', red-leather bindings, gladdened my father's heart. *Many Conventions . . . The World's Work. . . A Diversity of Creatures . . .* all bound limply in scarlet leather, printed on India paper with the elaborate title page, the elephant's device and the swastika: my father would sit, bolt upright in his armchair under a central hanging light, reading over and over again the Kipling short stories that stirred his imagination.

My father was a short-sighted man who dreamed of being a great soldier. He was an old-fashioned man who longed to serve his country. And Kipling, with *his* short-sight, his outmoded patriotism, was the magic key that evidently opened my father's heart to *his* own inner life.

When my father went to war in 1914 and led his battalion of the 6th Northumberland Fusiliers up a road towards the village of St. Julien under shell-fire, that inner world must have become too harsh a reality for him. For when my father came back from war he closed his mind to the world and its intrusions.

I loved my father deeply – but only since his death have I begun to have any understanding of the gay, imperious, romantic character who went so cheerfully to war and returned, uncomplaining but deeply shocked, to dive into the much more satisfactory world of books.

My father set me an example – of courage, of good manners, of gaiety. About the only obvious grip on reality that he had, in the forty years that I knew him, was to pay his bills meticulously, on the nail, cheerfully subtracting 10 per cent discount for prompt payment. People he loathed. Their chattering drove him dotty with boredom. 'I'm beastly deaf,' he would say, 'and don't care for social meetings.'

So our house, which should have been a cheerful place, filled with my mother's friends, revolved as silently as the great globe around the axis of a large, friendly, quiet man whose only way of dealing with visitors was to show them grimly to the door. 'Thank you so much.' 'Good morning.' 'What can I do for you?' How often, in my mind's ear, can I hear my father's voice saying these three simple phrases?

Mother's friends *did* get in, of course. They came to tea. They gossiped. I would lie face downward on the floor, reading (or pretending to read), while my ears picked up fragments about a Rosamond Lehmann, who had lately married a Mr Leslie Runciman and was fascinating the whole of 'Newcastle Society'.

Mother belonged to a tennis club, too, called Portland Park, which in those days was in Jesmond Road. Here wonderful snobbish attitudes were adopted. Portland Park called itself 'The Lords' and referred to a lesser, more plebeian club alongside it as 'The Commons' . . . Once a week there was a great tea given by one of the members, and when it was Mother's Tea Day enormous quantities of egg sandwiches were cut in the kitchen to be eaten by other female members, and I was allowed to eat the crusts off the bread, and the little bits of egg and mayonnaise.

The lawn tennis, I think, was of a pretty low standard compared with Wimbledon, but Mother was blissfully happy there and could never understand (in later years) why I went creeping off to join less socially acceptable clubs where the people actually hit the ball over the net.

Father was bored stiff by Portland Park: or indeed any people whom he met face to face. He greatly enjoyed *stories*, relayed to him by Mother, of the goings-on there, but he saw no reason to go and sit under a red May tree and sample the people for himself. 'I'm beastly deaf,' he would say, 'and very nearly blind, too.'

In fact Father was only deaf when he cared to be. Inside his ears (which he claimed had been damaged by the guns of St. Julien) there were tiny excluding curtains, which he rolled down at will.

His eyes were another matter. He really needed his

eyes, to read with. And when, in his late fifties and early sixties, he began to suffer from an obscure form of 'blistering' on the surface of the cornea he went into a nursing home and there underwent an operation to improve the condition. Quietly, gaily, he lay there in the dark with his eyes bandaged, learning, of all things, a long poem of almost complete decadence by Oscar Wilde called 'The Sphinx'.

I would visit him every day and read a quatrain. Father would gravely repeat it after me. By the end of the fortnight, in perfect harmony, the pair of us had learned the whole poem.

'In a dim corner of my room, for longer than my
    fancy thinks,
A beautiful and silent sphinx has watched me through
    the shifting gloom'

it begins, I remember. And it ends:

'False sphinx, false sphinx by reedy Styx, old Charon
    leaning on his oar
Waits for my coin. Go thou before, and leave me to
    my crucifix
Whose pallid burden, sick with pain, watches the
    world from wearied eyes
And weeps for every soul that dies. And weeps for
    every soul in vain.'

'Goodness, how cynical,' I said, shutting the book with a snap as we accomplished our task of memory.

'I don't care about the fella's sentiments,' said Father, defensively. 'It's the noise that the *words* make that I like.'

Words, words, words . . . yes, indeed. What an impact they made in that shadowy room, with Father lying happily on the bed and the pair of us reciting, murmuring the word patterns together.

When my father died I hunted round for something that would remind me of a relationship that had been so satisfactory to both of us. I found his nail scissors: how often I had borrowed them, and he had followed me shouting about the house: 'Give them back . . . Give them back . . .' And I found the privately printed edition of 'The Sphinx'. Looking through it the other day, touched by half-remembered, half-forgotten rhyming patterns and sprung rhythms, I came on Robert Ross's note at the beginning: 'The author always told me that it was composed and written in Paris, at the Hôtel Voltaire, Quai Voltaire . . .' The Hôtel Voltaire . . . Quai Voltaire. Evocative words. Immediately I felt that I was lying in the Piscine Deligny, in the hot Paris heatwave sun . . . golden-brown from the sun, half looking at the huge white thunder-clouds drifting over the River Seine. Walking slowly across the Quai to the Hôtel Voltaire for an aperitif, shaking hands with Madame Picot, whose restaurant stands on the Quai Voltaire.

Madame Picot is a small, tired-looking Frenchwoman, typical (you might think) of those Parisienne matriarchs who run bistros and have children and serve food and *bière* and wine behind a long, zinc counter and two huge urns. She is pale, peaky-looking. Her face lights up brilliantly when she shakes hands, as though an electric light had been switched behind her face. Her son is grown up now, and he serves with her in the restaurant. And when she greets me, pushing back a sleeve of her grey cardigan to do so, it is easy, seeing that brilliant smile, to remember that Madame Picot in her apparent frailty is as tough as old leather leggings. That brilliant smile conceals the fibres of France.

Above her, in the wall above our heads, is a plaque. It says that Voltaire died here. There is also a plaque that says that the Battle of Paris, which led to the liberation of the city from the Nazis, was planned here. Nazi officers fed and boozed on the ground floor, while Madame Picot, smiling, let the Resistance boys in by the side door. 'Those were brave days,' Madame Picot will tell you. 'Black and white days. Days when we knew who was friend and who was enemy.'

This is the reality of the Quai Voltaire. Yet around the corner Oscar Wilde, young and hopeful, once sat and scribbled and dreamed, drunk on beautiful words, and built himself an indestructible escape writing that poem 'The Sphinx'. He knew nothing of any unhappy reality to come. To be a writer is always to lie a little, to flirt with reality, to rearrange it.

Chapter Two

The Pegs That You Know

Reality has everything to do with knowledge. With knowledge of the truth, and therefore with 'education'. Education is everything you choose to make it. It is the broadening mind, the opened soul, the questing heart. Knowledge comes only to the lover, just as a great actor can only bring his role alive with affection.

The theatre *should* be a great medium of education. For example, Paul Scofield and Emlyn Williams, at different times and in different places leading men in *A Man for All Seasons,* Robert Bolt's play about More, lately achingly convinced me that Thomas More was a man who so adored life that even in the moment of his death he learned something.

I learned very little at my schools. Because I have a fast mind and an unusual memory I fooled the examiners. I knew all the time, and I bet they did too, that it was all a trick. My education has come to me since school, mainly by meeting people, by loving them, by work, by talking about other people's work. I have tried, and I have occasionally succeeded in doing so, to develop such gifts as I have been given.

One seeks out knowledge when one needs it. The important thing is to know where such knowledge can be found. Seldom in books. Dimly I was aware that 'teachers are only people after all', that books are only written by people after all. How could I learn anything from books? I could *enjoy* books. That was another thing entirely. Since I abandoned organised education I have scrambled after reality and truth (which I must remind myself should not be confused with knowledge), scrabbling away like some wretched ant-sized prospector at the side of a mountain with a child's bucket and spade. In spite of myself, with all my shoddy equipment, I have come up every now and then with some sheer gold-dust of pleasure and insight, usually as a result of a relationship with someone more gifted than myself.

Let me return to a typical example of such a gold nugget: Emlyn Williams. When I was a rebellious school-child, star-struck as only a girl of sixteen can be, I wrote to Emlyn and asked for his autographed photograph. I had seen him in *Night Must Fall* in the Theatre Royal, Newcastle, en route for the West End of London; I had seen him in a film called *The Case of the Frightened Lady*: I had seen the local rep perform *A Murder Has Been Arranged*. Obligingly he sent me a picture. For years I kept it, together with a highly coloured portrait of Greta Garbo on sateen which could be transferred to decorate something called 'a nightdress case' – oh, and a black and white glossy print of Marlene in a white uniform with froggings in *The Scarlet Empress*. Neither Deitrich nor Garbo signed theirs: their pictures meant less to me for this reason. There is an alchemy in an autograph.

Emlyn. I first got to know him in Paris, in a terribly grand apartment rented by Josh and Nedda Logan. I arrived there at a cocktail party one night (William Saroyan was there and Thornton Wilder too) late and idiotically giggling because of a ridiculous game I had been playing at *another* party with Noël Coward.

Noël and I had climbed to this other party up a fire escape, Noël ahead, me hurrying behind, calling out to him querulously, 'Don't go so fast, my little peg heels are getting stuck in the ironwork.' Noël sharply replied, 'The pegs that you know,' and I answered, 'Oo yes, Peggy O'Neill, Peg O' My Heart, Peg Woffington . . .' 'Chota peg,' said Noël, and abruptly finished the game, which was just as well, as the rest of *that* party thought that the Master had gone raving mad. (Three little Pegs – roast Peg.)

I confided all this to Emlyn.

'Oh, I *know,*' said Emlyn. 'Isn't it curious? I like the weather game, too – people with names, you know, weather-connected names.' He looked over at a chic guest. 'Carmel Snow,' he said.

'Marie Tempest,' said I.

'Robert Frost,' said Emlyn.

'Phineas Fogg,' I said.

'Doesn't count,' said Emlyn, 'he's a character in fiction. Claude Rains, Binnie Hale, Lesley Storm.' Again the rest of *that* party thought we had gone raving mad.

That was the year when Fellini's film *Dolce Vita* had obsessed me. Emlyn told me that it was too long for him and he had walked out at the end of the first half. 'I'm sorry,' I said, 'I can't love someone who did that to *Dolce Vita.*'

We met by chance next day, outside Fouquet's, and Emlyn hastened to say, 'I went back this afternoon and saw the second half absolutely fresh, and you're right, it *is* a marvellous, moving film.'

This flattered me deeply. Emlyn does not wear his heart on his sleeve or any other part of his clothing. His darting, biting, occasionally waspish, wit is beautifully contrived to protect his little boy's eagerness. Few people get under his guard. On the occasions when I have done so I have felt deeply privileged, just as (all those years ago) I was privileged by the autographed postcard. Emlyn's witticisms (and I have been there at the cataleptic birth of many of them) are the common currency of the theatre dressing-room and the tables at the restaurants where actresses and actors meet. But Emlyn's wild fantasy, his kindness, his glowing imagery: they are impossible to describe. Let me try. I was once in Emlyn's dressing-room in the A.N.T.A. Theatre in New York when he began to embroider an idea that Ernest Hemingway attended bull-fights *with* the bull, tucking him into his seat beside him in the stand, putting a straw hat on the bull's head, a cigar in his mouth, chewing gum, dark glasses:

'How else,' cried Emlyn, 'did Hemingway get his information? Of course he was a Friend of the Bull . . . Of course, of course . . .'

And all this was delivered at top speed, immediately after a tremendously tiring performance: delightful, wonderful, outrageous Emlyn, still (as one of his sons said of him) 'with the aspect of an elderly student'.

A student. Yes, indeed. And that is what I hope my aspect is, too.

There is only one thing I cannot forgive Emlyn. That he will not allow me to meet Miss Cooke, the remarkable woman who managed his education, helping him to acquire French, steering him to an Open Scholarship to Christ Church, Oxford, and who now lives in Leeds, alas, unvisited by me. She was the original for Miss Moffat in *The Corn is Green*.

How I wish at my last, most exclusive, girls' school in Brighton, Sussex, I had had a Miss Cooke to emulate. I longed with all my heart for *someone* to hero-worship: a hero, a heroine upon whom to model my personality, my character.

I can remember looking around me at that over-publicised school, faint with disgust at the prefects, the resident staff, the visiting specialists. For example, it wasn't possible, fond though I was of him, to fall in love with Mr Parkin, the fencing master who taught me to parry and thrust and riposte on Tuesdays. He wore a high-waisted overcoat and a bowler hat slightly on one side, and his face was mildly cut about with romantic duelling scars. Yet I could not form an attachment for him.

My instinct has always been a humble one. That was why I wrote to Emlyn and asked for an autographed photograph. And that was why this photograph (together with those of Dietrich and Garbo) represented Life to me. Garbo and Dietrich and Emlyn Williams were the sort of people I wanted to know, and who I dimly perceived were around in the world. If I studied and took pains I could develop myself along their lines . . .

The instinct to turn inwards and take refuge in my own mind became, at this school, an instinct of self-preservation. I could come to no real harm in there, dreaming of Emlyn's latest play, playing gramophone records of Miss Dietrich singing 'Johnny' and 'Mein Blonde Baby' and wondering what Miss Garbo thought about the League of Nations Union. It made me a little vague, of course, in my dealings with the rest of the community, since I was in heart and mind almost constantly elsewhere, walking in imagination along a sandy white beach with Emlyn in the South Seas, talking about Writing for the Theatre and what were His Plans for the Future? I very seldom, at that time, gave my own future a thought. (Nor do I now. Is that odd? I have never seriously considered I have a future at all.)

Dear me. How I disliked that anonymous school in Sussex. How unfortunate for my poor mother and father who sent me there, so hopefully and making such sacrifices to pay the fees, that I should have been so grim

in my rejection of it and all (as they say) it stood for.
I'm sure both my mother and father thought they were
doing their best for me. After all, before I went I was
a sickly child. And the health-giving air of Brighton is
notorious. As I grew healthy and put on weight and
escaped inwards, daydreaming, my subconscious and
unconscious mind was driven underground.

Curiously enough, there was beauty at that school
– endless, almost cloying, beauty: wind racing through
cornfields around our barbed-wire prison fence, comb-
ing back the corn like a woman's hair; the crescent moon
at dawn hanging low over the Palace Pier, the whisper
of the silken tide below the cliffs, rippling in along the
esplanade.

Of course I saw these things. I felt them, too. I had
enough sleepless nights to watch them from my window,
many afternoons to absorb the dazzling blue sky, the
cunning architecture, the horrors of 'chapel'.

How foolish of me, C. of E., baptised, confirmed and
all, to so dislike a place of worship: white marble, gold
inlays. It was like being asked to sit on a wedding cake
and think of higher things. Four white ensigns hung
there, flags of the British Royal Navy, which had flown
at the sterns of destroyers which my school had adopted
long ago, in World War I, at the Battle of Jutland.

Through the sermon I would keep my eye on the
flags and imagine ships. Ships have always tugged me
away, as islands do, as the mention of the very word
'Greece'. The sight of their masts, spars, swelling clean

lines pulled up on a beach; sliding away through deep water; standing, bobbing, roped like wild horses at a quayside: the thought of a ship, the name of a ship, is enough to send my mind off, out of the moment, into that inner secret world.

So I would sit through Matins, through adolescence, while someone thundered a voluntary on the foot keys of the organ – my eyes seeing rows of silent girls in their neat navy blue, their striped ties: my heart occupied with an empty beach, a bending pine tree, a blue horizon, somewhere, endlessly elsewhere.

I MUST GO DOWN TO SLOUGH AGAIN

In those days, of course, in my adolescent stupor I thought only in terms of dream islands. I had not, my childhood being sheltered, to say the least of it, suffered the experience of seeing a dream turn into a reality.

Years later, when I became a journalist, I discovered that to think is not necessarily to dream. And if I dreamed something it was more than likely to come true.

The most satisfactory dream of all still revolved around islands – islands and boats. Allow me to give you an example of an island dream coming true, in no uncertain way.

Once, about ten years ago, my partner Jonnie and I decided to spend a weekend in a boat on the river.

Jonnie, Joan Werner Laurie, the editor of *She* magazine, with whom I have lived for the best thirteen years of my life, is a character of great fascination. She is always perpetually, tirelessly, striving, expecting of others the near-impossible standards she sets on herself. She is, in my opinion, the greatest editor in London.

I can see her raise an eyebrow at that extravagant description. A kind eyebrow. For with all her perfectionism, which might otherwise make life with Jonnie a bit of an effort, morally and mentally, there goes kindness of heart, warmth of understanding and a sweetness of nature, which makes her drop anything, everything, at a moment's notice to help someone in distress. She despises people who don't try. She hates hypocrites. She loathes liars and pretentious idiots who play-act. She is the best company in the world and quite the most stimulating companion. To her, boats and companions and islands are delightful, exciting, physical adventures. She has all the pros and cons nicely weighed out in terms of wet feet and fine weather and speed in knots. I, alas, still see everything sloppily through a fog of romantic spars and masts dipping against a summer sky.

We hired the boat for our weekend from a large boating lady called, I think, Farmiloe. She looked us between the eyes and said, 'Call me Bunjie.'

In exchange for pound notes we became temporary masters of a small, hideously manœuvrable craft made of tin, which whirled about on the River Thames like a crazy mad water-beetle.

Because the boat was made of tin it was as light as a plastic saucer. The tiny tin cabin had a tiny tin floor, which acted as a powerful catapult. Anything I placed upon it, cups of tea, empty coffee tins that I might be using as chamber-pots, open tins of baked beans, would leap high in the air, drenching the cabin with tea, baked beans and so on, whenever I moved my weight. The craft was propelled by a powerful outboard motor. When Jonnie wanted to go astern she would swing it on its haunches. This scared me stiff. I am no mechanic. Rather than tangle with an engine I will paddle all day with an oar, as God intended. But Jonnie, who is full to the brim with logic, loves machinery, and she loved experimenting with this (to me) hostile animal. As I lay rigid in the cabin, afraid to move, she announced that she could gauge the strength of the tiny propeller against the strength of the current so accurately that she could keep the boat stationary in midstream.

It poured with rain. At one point I remember drifting wildly backwards under a huge stone bridge somewhere near Windsor, fending the boat off the piers with a boat-hook while Jonnie happily stripped the engine down. Thank goodness no other boat ran into us. But I feel this is only due to the fact that there were no other boats on the river that day because of the pouring rain.

Later, as the rain pattered on the tin roof with a noise like clanging cymbals, I made fast to a likely piece of tree and dossed down, damp but happy, for the night. Immediately a torch shone in my face. A very toff voice indeed said sharply: 'Move away from here. This is Crown property.' In my terror I was certain I had moored us to the Duke of Edinburgh.

You would think that such weekends are *not* the stuff that dreams are made on? But you are wrong. By the time my clothes were dry, and I was back on dry land, I could only remember the good bits. Even the clangour of rain on the roof turned into a tiny pattering, like small birds' feet. And the very next weekend we went to Kingston on Thames and bought a boat, made of wood, with absolutely immovable, non-catapultable, wooden floorboards. (They were a bit rotten, actually.) We christened this boat *The Tig* and we took out a river licence for her.

It was excessively exciting. Feeling like Katharine Hepburn in *The African Queen*, Jonnie and I prepared for our great voyage from Kingston on Thames to Chelsea.

Ten years ago is not really a long time. But I can still feel the mental anguish I endured on that trip when the foreign bodies (and there are always a great many of these in the Thames) collided with our propeller. When this happened a tiny brass rod called 'the shearing pin' broke. Jonnie plunged into the water and hauled up the engine, stripped down the propeller and fitted a new one. This happened *five times* between Kingston and Putney. At this point the tide turned and our engine wasn't strong enough to fight it, so we floated briskly backwards under the bridge to bump into the bank below Bishop's Park. Here a large crowd collected and began to play games.

'See 'ow far you can spit, Bert.' 'See if you can spit over the lady's 'ead.' 'Ow, sorry, lady.'

In the end the river police towed us ignominiously up to Chelsea Yacht and Boat Club, read us a short lecture on our folly and impudence and lack of river craft. And with immense kindness and humour helped us moor. And there *The Tig* stayed, rising and falling on the tide all one long, sunny summer.

Sometimes I walked round *The Tig* and scraped her sides with a little paint-scraper. Sometimes I crouched in the cabin (this was beautiful) and watched the barges going by, riding high in the water. Once, anyway, I sank dramatically with her because of my misunderstanding of a stopcock.

Then Jonnie, the realist, noticed the peculiar smell of the mud at low tide. 'It stinks,' she said. 'And it's all full of worms.' I had noticed in my unrealistic way that there was something wiggling under the soles of my feet when I plodded around, enthusiastic, with my little paint-scraper.

One day Jonnie somehow hauled *Tig* out of the water (how on earth did she do it? I simply don't know) and had her put in the front garden at our old house in Clareville Grove, Kensington. There she looked extremely odd. It was a very small garden, and *Tig* overhung it, bow and stern, to such an extent that one or two of our more drunken neighbours, returning late at night, went into smart hysterics and rang up the police. We were rather proud of *Tig* in the garden. We used to give directions about the house. 'You can't miss it,' we used to say. 'It's the only house in the street with a boat in the garden.'

But one day Jonnie wanted to plant some flowers in the garden. So we bought a piece of Garrick Island near Hampton Wick and there attached *The Tig*. On our plot there was a caravan. This piece of island cost £450 and the man who sold it to us thought he was selling us the caravan which was full of spiders. 'You can do anything there that you so desire,' he said, mysteriously showing us round.

We never really took to the caravan. But we loved the island. It faced Hurst Park on one side and Garrick's villa on the other. And even in retrospect it gives me a guilty secret thrill – my first island filled with secrets and delights and treasure hidden long ago.

We managed to raise the £450. By selling Christmas stories, if you please. Marvellous stories they were, at roughly £50 a time, with titles like 'Lady Caradine and The Last Trump', 'Dame Rebecca and the Christmas Cherub' and 'The Baby and the Astrolabe'. Jonnie used to think up the plots, I would write them. Jonnie would edit them, and then I would sell them to the *Tatter* or *Good Housekeeping*. It took us roughly six exhausting weeks to rake together £450.

Tig boat cost us £75, so altogether we had £525 of capital saved (or wasted, according to what sort of a mind you have) in this little enterprise. So long as we weren't there we looked on our property with joy and pride. Sometimes we called it 'our place by the river'. Sometimes we spoke of 'going to the island for the week-end'. Sometimes we said, 'Let's take a picnic tea down to Hampton Wick,' and from my study, when I should have been concentrating on work, my mind's eye would fill with the beautiful stretch of water by Hampton and I would see sailing dinghies darting across a reach, rippled and cat's-pawed by light winds in the setting sun.

When we actually got there, however, it was a little different. We were always afraid that 'Bodge' (Tom, Jonnie's younger son) would fall in the water and drown when we turned our backs. We were absolutely certain that Nick (her eldest) would fall in and drown with us looking on. And, of course, it usually began, somewhat monotonously, to rain.

We loved the weird tufty garden, and the lawn that grew so fast and the mad rock garden full of wild forget-me-nots. We even liked the rotting out-houses and the Elsan, the rusty lawn-mower and the enormous willow tree, where Nick perched with his fishing rod. We even grew fond of the spiders. I used to cut the lawn like a crazy thing, but it grew even faster than my hair, and it looked better long. So eventually I gave in, and let it grow. And then the winter 'set in'. And I'm sure the only people who were at all happy that winter were the spiders 'doing everything they so desired' in the caravan.

We toiled. We tried to make sense of it. But the island defeated us and went casually back to nature. So did *Tig* boat, sinking at every tide until she lay there, poor old *Tig* boat, her gunwales awash, slolloping under the willow tree.

So we sold our lovely island, for £500, together with *Tig* boat. We even had to throw in a typewriter to get the place off our hands, saying that I had written a thriller there called *The Kat Strikes*. So altogether (including the typewriter) I suppose we lost £50.

And Jonnie and I settled to a happy, island-free middle age. Until, of course, I went raving once more.

But this time about a *Greek* island, where the sun always shines.

Chapter Three

You Can't Put a Heifer on the Stage, Mrs Worthington

But these terrible revelations of dream-come-true were still ahead in my life. Locked in the clamp of childhood, my mind only concerned with imaginary and therefore blissfully beautiful landscape, I would have been as dismayed by reality as a young virgin might be appalled by the reality of sex. As I grew, fast and thick and healthy at my expensive, exclusive, anonymous girls' school in Sussex, and particularly in the holidays from that school, my mind would slip away into the half-world that God reserves for children, lunatics and drunken sailors.

From having been tiny and light and agile, like a minnow, I suddenly became all hands and hips and thighs. And in the holidays Mother tried to whack my subconscious mind awake with her maxims. Here are Mother's six best necessary rules to Social Life:

1. When at a dance don't get into a group, stand alone, so your good points (if any) can be recognised.

2. If all else fails get a plate of something and hand it round.
3. Patent leather draws the feet.
4. Don't look into a man's club, it's horrid.
5. Never catch an eye, it's not nice.
6. When sitting on a sofa with a man who is shorter than you are, wriggle around sideways and look up at him.

And I was *not* an apt pupil for these excellent Edwardian edicts. I was muscular indeed, seventeen years old and eleven stone, and when people ran into me on the lacrosse pitch *they* fell down. My neck was a thick column of muscle running out sideways to my shoulders (like those photographs of footballers sitting in striped jerseys with arms folded) and I looked simply appalling buttoned into the coffee-coloured lace that Mother had in mind. I was a sad disappointment, not only to Mother, but to myself. I knew that the role of young lady from the provinces was not for me.

At the age of seventeen I imagine I faced up to myself fair and square, with none of these nonsensical day-dreamings and evasions.

The only thing that everyone acknowledged I did well was to play games. Oh, and they admitted I had a good speaking voice. (John Laurie, the actor, had judged the poetry competition at school, had given me the prize and said so.) I was also, although nobody knew it, a good saleswoman. And, as I have described elsewhere, in a book called *Why I'm Not a Millionaire*, I became at seventeen a sports reporter, a radio actress (for the voice only, for you can't put a heifer on the stage, Mrs Worthington) and a commercial traveller in sports goods. Funnily enough, I was a big success in my triple role, a seventeen-year-old tycoon, every second of whose life was occupied. I had a syndicated sports column with different by-lines. I rehearsed big dramatic roles in the evening for one shattering transmitted live performance each week for the BBC: and the balance sheet of my sales of badminton shuttlecocks delighted the eye of the managing director of T. H. Prosser Ltd.

And you think all this would leave me with no time to daydream?

Don't you believe it. You see, I never quite believed in any of these activities. They made me quite a lot of money (particularly for a girl of seventeen, eighteen, nineteen). I managed to buy a small car. They could have made me independent of my father's house. But there was still a strong suspicion I was play-acting. I even thought I was play-acting myself.

When I played lacrosse in the trials for the North of England, or walked to the wicket against Lancashire at Chester le Street on August Bank holiday, I was someone else doing these things. N. Spain didn't flip the ball past the slips for a quick and easy single (cheerfully describing it all in the local paper next day, and getting paid for it, too). It was Bradman or Duleepsinjhi, all coordination and grace. The miracle is, daydreaming as I did, that I ever hit the ball at all. How did I make all those runs against Lancashire when I wasn't even *there*? When I wasn't even me?

And those lovely scripts that arrived for me through the post from the BBC, huge brown envelopes with a big sticker label on showing the lion holding a squirt of electricity in its naked paw – as I read those scripts I knew darned well I was playing at 'being an actress'. I felt precisely the same sensation of unreality flip through me the other day when I learned lines for a film called *Live It Up* (in which I made a fleeting appearance as 'Nancy Spain') and a Charlie Drake spectacular called *We Diet at Dawn* (ditto).

In the cast list, and on the slips of both these epics, it said: 'For newspaperman read newspaperwoman throughout.' So, in spite of the nice fee the film and the TV company paid me, I knew the whole thing couldn't be 'for real'. And that was how I felt studying Anne Marie, the heroine of *Fell Top* ('You're a hard woman, Anne Marie . . .' 'Ay, and who has taught me to be so? 'Tis thee, Jane Ellen, 'tis thee . . .'), and Grace Darling of *Longstone Light* ('Father! Father! There's a ship on the Harkers . . . !'). I was Dame Edith in her new comedy role, I was Dame Peggy, I was anybody at all except N. Spain . . .

And when I sold hockey sticks and rackets and shuttle-cocks from door to door, in the streets and clubs and schools of Sunderland and Newcastle and Hartlepool and Darlington, I knew darned well I wasn't me. Those powerful hands on the steering wheel of the car, that gentle persuasive voice, that quiet determination with secretaries and headmistresses that pattered on and on, that was Henry Ford in the making, or Nuffield, or Beaverbrook, I assure you. And even when I sat down in my attic bedroom at home (I who had been so hope-less at arithmetic at school) and found out that 12 per cent was considerably more than 10 per cent, and 5 per cent on tennis balls was hardly worth while bothering about; even when I squared my shoulders, and opened a bank account, and acquired a cheque-book and the other machinery of adult life – even when I did all this I still didn't believe a word of it. At the back of the mind of the great cricketer, sports writer, salesman, actress, would come that mocking question from some unin-volved part of me: 'Who the hell do you think you are?' Who, indeed? . . .

For example, I remember writing off for my first passport for my first holiday abroad. I was fascinated by the whole thing. Daughter of George Spain and Norah Spain I was, both British, and here was my birth certifi-cate to prove it. No problem. A doctor or clergyman or magistrate to witness the foregoing and risk his rep-utation as to whether this was the truth? No problem. Thirty-five shillings? Even this was no problem to that bursting embryonic tycoon, with its little bank account. Where, then, did the problem lie?

Well, when the passport arrived, clearly proclaiming that Miss Nancy Spain of the United Kingdom (Royaume

Uni de Grande Bretagne et d'lrlande du Nord) accompanied by 'his wife and by his children, Citizen of the United Kingdom and Colonies', was to be 'allowed to pass without let or hindrance' or else the Principal Secretary of State for Foreign Affairs, in the Name of Her Majesty, would like to know the reason why . . . here was the problem. Miss Nancy Spain, clutching her foreign currency, her huge yellow wallet from the A. A. *and* the pristine passport, Miss Nancy Spain was certain that she didn't exist at all.

The passport was good, though. There was a photograph of someone in it ('Hmm,' said my sister, 'a girl who would make a nice parlour maid') and many blank, unused innocent pages. Surely, surely, I thought, tucking it away into the yellow wallet, someone with a passport knows *who* they are, *what* they are doing and what they want to be? Proudly I had fingered the beloved thing. Nancy Spain was a journalist, it said, five foot six and a half inches high, with hazel eyes and brown hair. And the tickets and the A.A. routes proclaimed the fact that she was going to the South of France. I shelved the problem of identity for later.

WORLD WAR II, SO WHAT DO I DO FOR AN ENCORE?

The Road to the South, the NI to Paris, the N7 to the Mediterranean Sea, the Route Bleue. Ah, how often in my dreams have I taken it and listened to the poplars whipping by the open driving window: *whup*,

whup, whup. Why, the noise of the poplars is even more exciting than their flickering shadows, falling across the windscreen like an old silent jerky movie. Paris to Nevers, Nevers to the Valley of the Loire, the Loire to the Rhône. And then Avignon and the silence of the heat of the day, all the way down to the Delta of the Rhône, Cassis, Cannes, Monte Carlo: and then, if you will, the Italian Riviera, all the azure coast.

I first travelled this road in 1939, in the second-hand Ford I had bought for £75, the result of the tycoon's first big deal: in badminton shuttlecocks. In the boot of the car there was a tent and a groundsheet and a fly sheet. Beside me there was a huge hunk of French bread and a slopping bottle of warm wine.

I crossed the Channel in the ferry boat, because there was no Air Bridge in those days. I marvelled at the crane, swinging the car on board. I felt grown-up indeed, driving on the right, and when the rain and wind suddenly stopped, and the cold northern light became brilliant southern stuff, I was suddenly play-acting no longer. This was me. This was the real thing. There was no point in running up a quick dream or two to escape from this.

The heat hit me at Grasse. For some reason I had come over the Alpes Maritimes at that point, and I remember scrabbling, sweating, scratchy and determined on comfort, into my shorts in the back of the Ford under the amused stare of several French workmen.

The smell of the scent-flower meadows at Grasse. In their honey sweetness, in their warm baked-sugar-biscuit way, the flower meadows have always distilled the South for me. To stand there, as I did on that day in August, breathing in, it was a statement of all the things that existence can be. Within a month, as my instincts must have discerned, for I can remember being frightened by such happiness, all that sweetness was to be locked away behind the grey, flat doors of total warfare. And a way of life I had only glimpsed, a way of 'no responsibility', of carefree pagan joy, something I had always supposed just to be the 'dream' life, was to be forbidden to me for the duration of hostilities.

After that holiday, on 3rd September 1939, I went back to uniformity again, diving into the Women's Royal Naval Service and its navy-blue coat and skirt, without joy, and, anyway for the first four years, without rebellion in my heart.

But that was a long, sad war, lit here and there with flashes of danger and flashes of humour like a firework display: and it was carried on in cold, northern lands, far from the blue beaches. In certain songs, in gramophone records of unbearably saccharine loveliness, the glimpse I had of pine trees running down to the seashore, of sand unbroken by any footprint but my own, would return to me. 'J'attendrai' was such a song. But it was no lover that was waiting for me, night and day. It was an island. It was the South. It was escape.

I thought of this not long ago, as I twirled my hired Volkswagen caravan round the corners of the road to Marseilles from Avignon, listening out of the corner of one ear for the promised *whup, whup, whup* of the poplars and the hissing of the crickets like so many steam-pots on the boil. I was looking for a certain turn in the road where there was a workmen's cafe by a canal, where I drank my wine and ate my bread in 1939. Of course, there was no such café – it was only in my mind's eye.

In 1939 I wasn't rich. (Nor am I now.) And my mother was furious that I had decided to holiday abroad. She was convinced there would be a war. 'All the more reason to go, then,' I said, obstinately loading my tent into the car. 'There won't be another chance.'

Nor was there, so far as I was concerned, until 1955.

In the thirties camping in France wasn't quite as well organised as it is now. Here and there were places still where human foot seldom trod, beaches that were deserted as the sun.

So I drove to a coastal village somewhere between Agay and St. Tropez and sought out a local dignitary, and he, wiping his mouth after a very good lunch (with a good deal of wine and garlic in it by the smell of his breath), led me to the butcher's where I hired a field for a week. I remember being very pleased because the butcher said I looked like Queen Elizabeth, now the Queen Mother. It was only later, when he was savagely hitting a tin of ham with a huge meat-cleaver, and I was reeling back from him, that I decided he must be a little tight.

For fifteen shillings a week I became tenant of a meadow that stretched along the last of the solitary beaches in the South of France. At one end the pine trees slid down to the water. There was a dried-out river bed, heavily thatched with bulrushes and osiers. And clover, the last crop of hay, and a wilderness of buttercups, daisies and tiny purple wild orchids, growing in a sandy soil into which it was almost impossible to knock a tent peg.

However, I put up my tent.

There were three days of perfection, of sun, and sleep under the stars (amazing that they were the same stars as England and I could clearly see the Plough and Orion striding over the village lights), and swimming to keep cool, and wine kept in the shade without ice, and hot rolls bought in the village and wolfed in the cool of the morning before the weather went mad.

I was walking down the village street one day, rather pleased with a pair of shorts I had bought from a stall in the market for five shillings, when I saw a whirling corkscrew of dust in the distance. Men and women were running from it, doors were banging, children running, stalls overturning. It was a little hurricane.

And hot on its heels came one of the most electrifying thunderstorms I have ever seen. Pink lightning. Sky dark as midnight. Rain in hot sheets. Lightning jagging, forked, around the car, held at bay only by the rubber tyres. Thunder like a perpetual roll of drums, coming at the same second as the lightning. The tent flapping like a pocket handkerchief. The dry river bed suddenly a raging torrent: beige, angry growling water with white flecks of foam curled on the surface.

I took refuge in an hotel. I remember the revelation of the taste of the lobster. Until that day I had only eaten camper's food. I had no idea that food could taste so good. And I remember the lightning far away across the Mediterranean flickering towards Africa. In the morning I went to look at my beach.

The torrent had cut it in two. The sand was churned up from end to end. In the edge of the tideless sea, brought down from God knows where, floating in three feet of water, was refuse enough to put one off the tideless Mediterranean for life. Dead cats, old bicycle wheels, tin cans, broken bottles, a mess that was too much for *me*.

I might talk of symbolism.

Three weeks later we were at war. A year later France had fallen and that whole coast had become the shabby refuge of 'Unoccupied France'. I knew nothing of this, of course.

In my ignorance, in my cold northern days and nights I still imagined that coast unchanged, unharmed. As I sat in my cab (I was a lorry driver by then and responsible for delivering naval stores and rum and ammunition and anything else Their Lordships so decreed) I could only visualise that shimmering horizon and smell the resin in the trees. In my heart the beach was always deserted. I saw no people, no refugees, no thunderstorms, no dead cats, no rusty bicycle wheels. I only saw three hundred yards of curving, perfect sand, heard the warm waves lapping and felt the silence of the South under the sun, waiting for me like a constant lover.

Chapter Four

From N. Spain of Newcastle to Spain and Laurie (Exploitation) Ltd of London

'N Spain' left school, went to war, wrote a book about it called *Thank You, Nelson*, wrote a detective story called *Poison in Play* and so set herself up as an author in one London bed-sitting room after another. There, by mischance out of financial insecurity, a trouser-wearing character named 'Nancy Spain' was born: a character who had as little to do with the N. Spain I knew when young as the old cow has to do with the little heifer. I have now, as it happens, more or less given up wearing pants for public life. They are still the most comfortable, indeed the only reasonable, wear for an author or journalist who sits at a desk most of the morning, pounding on a typewriter. But because of the miracles of video tape I am sometimes able to watch the character named 'Nancy Spain' on the screen and the effect, the suggestion, of those pants was (I thought) displeasing.

Watching this television character, I have to admit, vaguely, that she is related to me. I must acknowledge her, dimly, as I might a rather repulsive cousin. I can see the family likeness breaking through, hear the tricks of the voice, all confusingly repellent. Because of the confusion I find it hard to watch a 'taped' show. I would like to do Madam over and give her a new face: new everything.

But in the days, nearly thirty years ago, of which I write 'Nancy Spain the Telly Phony' existed only in the publisher's contracts as 'Nancy Spain . . . the author'. ('Hereinafter called the Author' somebody always types, or prints, in the very first clause of all.)

'Nancy Spain . . . the author'. I suspect her of play-acting, too. She sat in her bed-sitting-room in Kilburn, self-consciously filling up special notebooks. There was a special notebook for 'dialogue overheard', a special pencil for writing dialogue fast. There was a magic and very, very pleasing fountain pen that wrote smoothly when describing landscape, another fountain pen which wrote the emotional stuff that journalists, amongst themselves, call 'Guff-guff'. And the author was particularly keen on the gesture used by *real* novelists (Monica Dickens said so), that of screwing up a page of paper into a ball and throwing it into the waste-paper basket in apparent disgust.

At the end of a thousand words N. Spain would rise to her feet, dust off her trousers, brush the crumbs from her lap (a very satisfactory thing, eating at work) and go for a little stroll, or a ride on a bus, to clear the exhausted imagination. On the bus: dreams of the characters in the novel and what they would do next. A peaceful, selfish, hardly human, existence, scarcely real. A hypnotised, half-drowned N. Spain who ate and slept and walked and talked and occasionally answered the telephone to a call from Newcastle from her mother, but otherwise knew no one, had contact with no one, and even saw the people in shops as sleepily swooning fish in a dim aquarium.

Nancy Spain was now a novelist. It said so in her new passport, that passport that was carefully kept up to date, in case one day there should miraculously be enough money to spare to make that journey to the South once more. Incidentally, it is worthy of note that certain places (like Tangier) find novelists more impressive than journalists: and other places (like the USA) find journalists more impressive than novelists. It is all a matter of financial dependence. So the current edition of Nancy Spain has both 'journalist and novelist' written on her passport to cover every contingency. Once, faced by an angry little Japanese gent bouncing in the Customs at Tokyo, I was asked, 'Why have you this national status of VIP?' and fell back stunned, saying, 'No, I haven't, have I, really?' which didn't help the Japanese at all.

But in those days I, the novelist, was filled to the brim with literature. I read books on The Novel and took literary reviews seriously and had an 'A' subscription to The Times Library. And on my shelves there were presently seven or eight detective stories bound up in blue and silver (as near a uniform edition as this novelist will ever get, I think) with the name 'Nancy Spain' clearly dye-stamped on the spine. So these novels were written by someone, albeit someone with no sense of achievement and very little money.

Occasionally, obviously, there were deep moments of satisfaction and self-confidence. Once or twice I managed to make a good joke, and I sat at the desk laughing and falling about with pleasure, wondering if ever anywhere some reader would share the joke with me. And once or twice I was overcome by a good review in some obviously trustworthy newspaper, which definitely existed, like the *Sunday Times*. So perhaps Nancy Spain was for real, after all.

Certainly London was real to me. London in 1945 was a marvellous thing. I was happy simply to breathe the London air and be a part of its wild life. I shared it with the pigeons, the sparrows, the rats and the mice who were such Londoners they made me feel positively provincial. I *was* provincial, after all. I learned to cook my own meals. I deeply resented washing them up. I walked in the parks in a voluptuous haze of gratitude to God that London was still there, after the Blitz, the buzz-bombs and the V2s, and that I was a Londoner. I thought I *was* a Londoner, my address surely proved it.

I didn't mind if it rained. When the sun shines in London the beauty is almost past bearing. The trees in Berkeley Square, throwing pools of dappled shade around the sly white statue: the trees are charming. They are even more charming in rain, particularly spring rain.

And the back streets of Soho, the embankment where H.M. Ships *Discovery* and *President III* and *Chrysanthemum* (flagship of Rear-Admiral Reserve Fleet) rub, tide by tide, creaking up and down: they are as good in the rain as the sun. London feeds my soul, the soul of someone who has never really escaped the northern birth right: warm hearts, rigid brick streets, cold winds, desolation of landscape, abandoned pit-heads, shipyards where grass grows, a river made dirty by men who made too much money too quickly.

All the London parks whisper in my heart under the London drizzle. The Green Park, where the lilacs follow the tulips so fast I often forget that spring has been. St. James's, where the lake lies smooth as silk behind the ducks and I once heard a man say, wonderingly, throwing crumbs to the sparrows, 'Like mice they are, look at them scrambling there.' And Hyde Park, with the Row and the clatter of horses' hoofs. Hyde Park seems to me a winter park, iron-bound in icy January as though hungry wolves linger by the Serpentine. Regent's Park, summer park filled with roses. I always go quickly by the zoo in case I should see a tiger in a cage among the roses. Everything in London delights me, from Clapham to Kilburn.

So why should I want to leave?

I never want to leave. It is only lately, when I occasionally become exhausted by the tumult of the telephone, that I find myself thinking wistfully of the warm beaches where I might perhaps lie and recharge my run-down batteries.

Jonnie it was, of course, who rescued me from bed-sitting-room life, from years of mismanagement and debts, from unpaid rent and that curious disease known as 'novelist's falsehood'. With her N. Spain became a Limited Company, 'Spain and Laurie (Exploitation) Ltd.', and moved into a series of well-run, haphazard, relaxed homes, with Jonnie's two sons, with Jonnie's astringency and sense of humour. I think that from the moment N. Spain became a company director she never really play-acted again. For her co-director, Jonnie, finds attitudinising and posing such a dreadful bore that such qualities cannot really live long beside her.

I once asked Jonnie if she wouldn't really rather like me to be trying to write great books that got good notices?

'Good heavens no,' she answered. 'It would be very difficult indeed to live with. *That* little black cloud of temperament moving round the house? No, thank you very much . . . over my dead body.'

Dear Jonnie. How much 'the Company' owes you. Under the guidance of Jonnie's quiet judgement N. Spain became editor, literary editor, book critic and finally a columnist and general reporter. And TV personality. And lecturer. And to a reporter, to the Spain of 'Spain and Laurie', realism is all. It is not so much that the romance has gone. It hasn't gone. The romance is still there. Spain and Laurie Ltd. do not *romanticise,* that's all.

By 1956, for example, when *Why I'm Not a Million-aire* was published, I had become a bit of a celebrity in

England. *Why I'm Not a Millionaire* created quite a stir. Christina Foyle gave a lunch for me, studded with millionaires at the top table. Lord Beaverbrook allowed me to review my own book in the *Daily Express*. And the Grand Order of Water Rats, Kings of the Music Hall, invited me to be guest of honour at their annual banquet and ball at the Dorchester.

Fresh from the Foyle Luncheon (which had been a great success) I togged myself up in all my finery and hung around waiting for Brian Michie to escort me. He arrived, looked spiffing in his black tie. I looked spiffing in my ball dress. As we left the house, full of champagne, Jonnie came to the gate with us.

'Listen,' she said. 'Remember the Holborn Empire.'

'Remember *what?* I asked, bewildered.

'The Holborn Empire,' she repeated. 'You know. That very famous music hall that they pulled down. If you get stuck, just fall back on that.'

I stood still on the pavement. Brian called to me to hurry up. He was already inside the taxi, bouncing impatiently up and down.

'But what has that got to do with me?' I asked, already striking an attitude. 'I am the woman of the year. I am the guest of honour. I am ... I am ...'

'Never you mind all that,' said Jonnie, gently. 'They are music-hall people. Remember the Holborn Empire. It is something that is bound to go well. Marie Lloyd. That should go well, too. Those two names mean a lot to them.'

'What was she saying?' asked Brian, as I joined him in the taxi.

'Oh,' I said, vaguely, 'she was just wishing me luck.'

We drove up, in style, to the ballroom entrance. We were received by King Rat, Prince Rat and their ladies. Everyone looked smashing. Brian and I perched on the corner of a sofa. Someone introduced us as 'Mr and Mrs Brian Michie'. We were startled. Then we went in to dinner. Then I ate my dinner, gulping away beside Prince Rat. Then someone stood to introduce me. And I suddenly, joyously, almost ecstatically, realised that Jonnie, my partner, was so dead right. There wasn't a Water Rat that had ever heard of *me* at all.

Now I had to speak. Up I got. I started shouting away into the microphone. My little jokes fell damp and flat, like coins in the gutter to a man who still eternally grinds his barrel organ when you want to remove him to the next street. Dead silence. Finally, in some agony, I flung the words 'Holborn Empire' across the ballroom. There was a burst of applause. Some cheering. Startled, I said them again. It was now quite clear to me that the Water Rats and their ladies had not even been listening. This time the cheering was prolonged. So I threw in 'Marie Lloyd' for good measure. Then, hell, I thought, let's stop while the going is good. So I sat down.

I then became aware that my petticoat had fallen off.

I stepped out of it, sneaked out of the side entrance, went home. And that was the end of 'Nancy Spain – the Woman of the Year'.

Make no mistake about this, if I am famous now I find that fame no burden. The people who come up to me at the Parthenon in Athens, in the Champs Élysées in Paris, even in New York and in Washington D.C., particularly when they ask for an autograph: why, I love them for it. I am delighted that 'Nancy Spain' has passed into rhyming slang and now stands as 'a drop of Nancy' for a 'drop of rain'. But I am so scared of sliding back into the bad old habit of asking who the hell I think I am that I am always masochistically enchanted with someone who doesn't know.

For example. There was a delirious encounter about five years ago when I was sitting at Wheeler's (fish restaurant supreme) next door to a merry little lunch party.

The party consisted of Jane Gaskell, then a seventeen-year-old novelist who had just had her first book published, Mrs Rae Jeffs, at that time publicity manager of Hutchinsons, my own English publishers, and Mrs Penelope Gilliat, now Mrs John Osborne, at that time features editor of *Vogue*. Penelope was telling Jane Gaskell how she would be 'taken up' by literary journalists. (I was at that time Lord Beaverbrook's book critic on the *Daily Express*.)

'No doubt you will meet Nancy Spain,' said she.

'What's she like?' asked Jane Gaskell, admitting in the same breath that she listened to me on *Woman's Hour*.

'Pathetic, really,' said Penelope. 'Always trying to get into night clubs in those trousers and getting thrown out –'

'You mean that she is very insecure, really?' began Jane Gaskell.

'Oh yes, indeed,' began Penelope. 'And what is more –'

I rose to my feet, charmed, and firmly joined the table.

'Now,' I said, 'I am going to buy you all strawberries and cream.'

Penelope's mouth fell slowly open, for I think she was the hostess.

'And who might you be?' she asked.

Rae Jeffs and Jane Gaskell both stared.

'Why, this is Nancy Spain,' they said in unison.

There was, I promise you, no offence in any of this. Next week Penelope came to lunch with me, in the Caprice, and she had a notable feast, with every dish named for her: 'Bombe Surprise de Penelope' and so on. We got on extremely well, and we always have done so, on all the occasions when we have met since then. But I would like to put on record (as if it mattered) that I have never tried to get into a night club in jeans, nor been thrown out of one. I cordially loathe night clubs and only go to them in the course of duty, as a columnist. When I do I ring the manager first to find out if I shall be welcome and what he would like me to wear. When I was a novelist I found I kept cleaner in trousers and a shirt, and then when I suddenly was saddled with them as a mark of identification I was genuinely surprised. I didn't think anyone was looking. But then I overheard another conversation, in a shoe shop, when a lady (who hadn't recognised me any more than Penelope had done) said sneeringly to a little girl, 'Now you don't want to grow up to be a Nancy Spain, do you?' and I began to think about it all.

It really was a bit sluttish of me to go on wearing these comfortable clothes. Perhaps I ought to stop. So I put on a skirt, for auditions and things. And a year or two ago a day came when I was sent for to audition a TV show with the late Maurice Winnick. It was called *Twenty Questions* and I had misheard my agent, April Young, on the telephone. *I* thought she had said 'Any Questions?' or even 'Many Questions?' and I was in a rare old lather of terror. So I went into Wheeler's as usual to calm down, and a man came over and kissed me. Quite an attractive man, too. (Let me add point to the story. That week we had all been reading and enjoying Jeanne Heal's adventures as a bus conductress in the *Evening Standard*.)

I had no idea who the man was, but I was delighted that he seemed to know me. We sat side by side at the marble bar, laughing and talking, eating oysters and swilling champagne, until he suddenly remarked, '"Ronnie Boy, Ronnie Boy," they said to me, "we'd like another of your Shiner farces."'

The penny, amazingly enough, dropped. I realised, with my quick and ready wit, that I must be talking, all unawares, to Ronald Shiner. As I came to my senses he slid down from his stool, kissed me warmly again and said:

'Well, bye-bye, Jeanne. Nice talking to you. That

was great stuff you wrote in the *Standard* about being a bus conductor. Great. Why don't you turn it into a film script, eh? Think it over. Good stuff, eh?'

And then he was gone, to his rehearsal. And I slowly went on, to my audition.

But I also must confess I love vulgar recognition, particularly from drivers and roadmen. I like them shouting out to me, 'Wotcher, Nance, old girl?' and 'Orl right, then, Hit or Miss? Ha, ha, ha.' In the days when I was suffering from a late attack of 'Who the hell do you think you are?' I acquired a huge white Ford Zephyr with my name spelt out in front. I adored this car.

But one day I crashed it. And whether it was the bang on the head or not, my attitude towards publicity and self-advertisement suddenly changed. I don't quite know why. Perhaps I prefer to creep around anonymously in the hopes that God's thunderbolt intended for N. Spain will fall somewhere else.

Before this crash I was quite shameless.

Raymond Way, my dear friend, who has made a million out of buying and selling such second-hand cars, helped me to 'personalise' the Zephyr.

He painted it chocolate-brown below to match its brown hood. This went up and down by electricity, like some strange animal snapping its jaws at the following traffic. He took the spare wheel out of its hole in the boot and mounted it on the back, in imitation of a 'Thunderbird', and he wrote 'Nancy Spain' in facsimile signature in gold all over it. And on the front, with an

'N' from Consul and an 'S' from Consul and a 'P' from Zephyr and an 'A' and a T from Zodiac and another 'N' from another Consul he spelt out 'N. Spain'. Shocking.

But when I bowled along, in this over-comfortable car, with the radio playing and the hood snapping up and down, I was pretty sure that I existed. Even when it rained I was in another world. Soft music from the radio. Warmth from the heater. What more could I ask?

And then this beloved car also saved my life.

Driving home along the Dover Road one dark October evening I fell asleep at the wheel from sheer exhaustion. The car turned a double somersault. Because it was a damp night I had the hood up. The hood took the full impact. Also, I was wearing a lambskin coat, known to Jonnie as 'old filthy', and as I clung to the steering wheel this noble garment absorbed the shock that must have hit my breast bone. Apart from a fair bruise, and the fact that I can bring back nothing of that day and evening before the crash (I can remember the radio programme that was playing, something with the George Mitchell Singers and that's all), I apparently clambered from the wreckage unscathed. I knew nothing of this. I woke in Dartford Hospital to find a young policeman sitting by my bed, remarking: 'Lucky to be alive you are. You usually pick 'em up dead off Death Hill.'

The self-advertising 'N. Spain' and 'Nancy Spain' all over the car had quickly identified me. Someone had fetched an ambulance. And everyone settled down to telling me how lucky I was to be alive.

'Lucky to be alive.' I most certainly am. No day has gone by since that date that I haven't thanked God for it. Not often on bended knees. I am really not a bended-knee type of girl. But often walking in the streets, particularly on a fine autumn day in a great city, with blue sky above the houses and the sun like a golden coin uprising, I have found my heart overflowing with pleasure and gratitude at the sheer simple act of life.

I had ample time to give thanks to the Lord that winter. Almost immediately my doctor and I discovered the reason for my exhaustion was that I needed, urgently, an operation for fistula and piles.

Of all the unmentionable, trivial and exquisitely painful things the anal operation comes top of every surgeon's list. It is also, because of its very nature, a screamingly funny joke.

Christmas Day that year I spent in the London Clinic with huge tears of self-pity welling in my eyes. A bright young curate pounced in through the door, carrying a little Do-It-Yourself kit for Holy Communion. I was too tired to do anything except accept (I hope gracefully) his Absolution and the words of comfort. I was awfully pleased when the door shut behind him. And lo and behold! he pounced back. This time he was dressed in grey flannels with a college scarf swathed round his throat. And he asked for my autograph. From this moment, when my self-pitying tears turned to weak tears of laughter I clambered back to rude health. And the *Daily Express* popped a cherry on top of the sundae (or parfait) of horror by appointing me their film critic. I adored this job, and it is still my ambition to be somebody's film critic. But it seemed to me to be adding insult to injury to have to sit on my wound in various West End cinemas, popping back to the London Clinic twice a day to have it dressed. For quite a while I lived in the clinic and used it as my home. A very strange way of life indeed.

Eventually, of course, I left the *Daily Express* and joined the *News of the World*. A great Sunday newspaper never produces the sort of tensions produced by a daily. And the more relaxed attitude in the offices in Bouverie Street exactly suited my new state of mind.

No more, I promised myself, would I allow my profession to deteriorate into a grind, a drag. No acquaintanceships, no friendship, would become chaotic and destructive. Each day, which, I had had so clearly pointed out to me, could easily be my last, was going to be fun once more.

40 MILLION FRENCHMEN CAN BE WRONG

To feel 'good' two things are necessary for me. I need friends who 'take me out of myself' and constant changes of scenery that relieve the 'deadline'. For quite a while, during and after that time when I felt I had been banged on the head both within and without, I used as my constant island of escape, my flight from pressure: my friendship with Ginette Spanier and her husband Dr Paul-Emile Seidmann. And with them I developed an uneasy relationship with the city of Paris, France, where they live.

'If you have one friend in your life on whom you can rely,' my father used to say, 'that's more than most of us deserve.'

My father also used to say, 'The world is run by fear and greed,' sitting comfortably in his chair in his nursery in Newcastle upon Tyne. His pessimism about humanity, his deafness, his modesty and reticence, all I am sure arose because of his experiences in World War I. And he withdrew from life almost to the same degree as I now run to meet it. I embrace where he turned from all its horrors, betrayals, triumphs, disloyalties, delights and revelations of affection.

Even landscape can betray one. Even the beloved South of France did not spread her magic ointment on Jonnie and myself one holiday when her two sons joined us. Instead of ten days of relaxed charm and inactivity, dreamily swigging wine and drowsily regarding the beautiful Belle Plage and our new friends, the Rappenaus, who run it, we found that it could be a long struggle with mosquitoes and sunburn and endless instructions for children on 'How to Live'. Neither Jonnie nor I are the missionary type, and it became increasingly clear that the sun was too strong for our darlings, who moreover did not awfully want to lie quietly there and didn't like wine. And we began to long for the day when we could return them both to base.

And I, because of Ginette, had discovered that there was a different view of the South that one could take. Ginette *loathes* the South of France.

Ginette Spanier is now Directrice of the House of Pierre Balmain, the famous couturier of Paris. Small and dark, with a heart as big as the aero port at Orly, she was born in Paris in the 17th *arrondissement* and brought up in Golders Green. Her father, Max Spanier, delighted her in the twenties when he lost his fortune. She was delighted because this meant that she could go to work in Fortnum and Mason in Piccadilly. Ginette is a born saleswoman. I doubt if she has her equal on earth. She sells all day long: for breakfast, dinner and lunch, and particularly at cocktail time. *Then* she keeps open house for every stray actor and actress or visiting fireman in Paris. Here, in her warmth and enthusiasm, she actually mends the souls of lonely tourists.

She married Paul-Emile Seidmann in 1939. Paul-Emile is tall, handsome, elegant, with short-sighted grey eyes and a sweet smile. He is now sixtyish, with the red ribbon of the Legion of Honour in his buttonhole, and about as distinguished a man as you will find. He mildly runs his professional medical life from an *appartement* in Paris, where he is quite likely to find Marlene Dietrich asleep on the consulting-room couch, Group Captain Townsend waiting in the drawing-room and Noël Coward in the spare bed. Oh, and Sir Laurence Olivier in the bathroom. Paul-Emile (Polly Mill, as Vivien Leigh calls him) seems to enjoy all this in his quietly sardonic way, and in between whiles he even manages to examine a patient or two. But in 1939, when he married Ginette, World War II began and France blew up.

When France fell and the French Army capitulated, Paul-Emile (who was a doctor in the Army) and Ginette crossed after a series of misadventures into the Unoccupied Zone. They lived for a while in Nice and nearly starved. I suppose this was the unhappiest time of Ginette's life, and I lived through it with her when she was writing her book *It Isn't All Mink.*

That any place could make someone suffer so much! I looked on the South of France with new eyes. That this beloved coastline, that Bay of the Angels, those capes and bays, the red rocks of Agay, the blue sea, the scintillating horizon . . . could only mean to Ginette a series of green crosses, representing chemists' where she had sold cotton goods as an angry, hot commercial traveller, trying to keep her husband and herself alive. This was a revelation to me. Where Jonnie and I had sat in different restaurants, sampling various *Soupes aux Poissons,* eating the fried fish of the Gulf, stuffing down *rouget* with fennel in its stomach, Ginette had gone temporarily blind from near starvation, Paul-Emile had had his professional status taken from him. Under the Nazi and Vichy regime no French-Jewish doctors were allowed to practise. Because Ginette and Paul-Emile were Jewish they lived in constant fear of denunciation.

And this was that same South of France.

Now, for a time I saw through Ginette Spanier's eyes the South of France. This disenchantment didn't last for long but while it lasted it seemed very real. And for a time all the light and the warmth and the twitter of the crickets; and the fireflies darting in the evening; and the sighing waves falling upon the beaches; and the sun . . . these things were suddenly no longer an escape for me. Instead I turned to the City of Paris; beautiful, tricky, fascinating and endlessly absorbing: a city with which to have a love affair. I never truly achieved this, but I can honestly say that Paris and I are still very good friends. The other cities in my life are Newcastle upon Tyne and London.

Chapter Five

Paris: I Kiss Her Left Bank

Newcastle upon Tyne has always been reality to me. My main root is there, drawing strength from my rebellion against middle-class provincial society, against the giving and taking of merchandise in marriage, the pathetic routine of bridge party and back-biting, jealousy and 'keeping up with the Joneses'. I am actually quite fond of the people who manage to pass their existence in this way, and at their best they have a wonderful vision of family life and the securities resulting from it. At their worst? Oh boy. Don't let's mention it.

And the North Country working class have always been my heroes and heroines. In the rain and cold, battling with futile courage against impossible odds, grimly building (on a diet of starch) a family. A family against the boss, against the system, against the unfairness of being born without talent. With only the white northern sky over them, the privy in the yard, the slag-heaps behind them, and in front of them the total greed which controls the future of the shipbuilding industry and the North-East. I know I am in danger of romanticising these men and their women, and their blind obstinacy in staying put, jobless and unyielding, living like slobs on the dole in the only place that is real to *them*. But I love them deeply, with all their faults.

And London is real to me as well. Here are lesser roots, 'sucker roots' I put down in my youth and arrogance and faith, suckers that still draw inspiration and strength from the streets, shops, parks, gardens, eating houses: and, best of all, my own and Jonnie's kitchen. The rich London way of life: the sauntering, casual, leisurely progress up and down Bond Street, looking in windows like Asprey and Cartier, flirtations with art galleries, this life is not really for me. This is a life that demands beautiful clothes, in the same way I have always supposed spoiled women demand jewels of their lovers.

My day, my life, is rum indeed if you analyse it.

It begins around 6 a.m. when I write my material for the *News of the World*, and for the various magazines who have me under contract. By 7 a.m. we have all breakfasted, by 8.30 a.m. I have waved goodbye to Jonnie and to Sheila Van Damm, who also shares our home. Then I am ready to type my rough draft, clearly and sweetly for the editor's eyes. By 10 a.m. the telephone has begun to ring like a crazy fire alarm, and by 11.30 a.m. my nerves are usually so tight strung that I have to have a hot bath to calm down and get ready for lunch. At this point I usually take the receiver off, because I find it is idiotic to leap from hot water, leaving wet footprints all over the carpet, except in answer to the imperious summons of my two agents – April Young of Kavanagh Productions Ltd. (who looks after my TV and radio bookings) and Ernest Hecht of Souvenir Press and Euro-Features Ltd. (who manages all my magazine contracts).

Both April (plump, sweet, kind and imaginative) and Ernie (sharp, lean, passionate for football and gay with all his success) know me very well indeed, and they know the hours I keep, so they usually reserve their telephone calls until 5.30 in the evening. They never, if they can help it, drag me damp and wrapped in a bath-towel to the telephone.

By 12 noon I am on my way to the *News of the World* or to the magazine with my copy in my hand, or with my copy sliding about on the seat of the car beside me. By 12.30 p.m. I have usually worked out answers to the voluminous mail and left Gloria Prior typing them. (Sometimes I leave poor Gloria high and dry with the mail for a week or two, and then she becomes a faint and plaintive voice on the telephone.)

By 1.30 p.m. I am usually lunching with some business date, by 3.30 p.m. I am keeping an appointment, recording a script at the BBC or dashing home to change for an evening performance.

With such a life London is hardly a resort to me. I love it. I love work. But often months can pass by before I can even get to a cinema. I seldom go to the theatre unless I have to write a story about it. My days of romanticising about the London theatre are long since over: or at least I think so. I did go mad one year and put £1,500 into a musical called *Little Mary Sunshine*. But that is another story.

London is my home. I could not live anywhere else. It has my heart and is my true love for always. But in the early stages of my passion for Paris I couldn't fail to see the contrast between the tension of my London day and the supernatural relaxation of my day in Paris. So I had time to observe the avenues, boulevards, quais, chestnut trees, the green of the Bois de Boulogne. And I could not fail to observe them through a fog of romance.

I never dreamed that I could ever become familiar with Paris, or ever learn to speak French. But that indeed is what happened. From being 'in love' with Paris I passed through seven years of change and began to 'love' her. Particularly when I began to work for the French magazine *Elle*. I suppose I had put down 'suckers' in Paris as well as London.

My day in Paris begins around 8.30 a.m. in the Queen Elizabeth Hotel in the Avenue Pierre Premier de Serbie. Then I ring down for croissants and coffee and a boiled egg. Then I talk to Monsieur Rambaud, the concierge, white-haired, elegant and trim in his exquisite frock-coat. We 'tutoyer' each other like mad, Monsieur Rambaud and I, and when we take farewell, or greet each other, we kiss each other on both cheeks.

In front of the Queen Elizabeth Hotel, on the sky-line, is the Church of Chaillot. Round the corner in the Avenue Marceau is the American cathedral. So the air of a Paris weekend is filled with the sound of bells, with a carillon that plays (rather badly) 'Eternal Father Strong to Save' and the mild snarling of French traffic. This starts up at 4 a.m. when the lorries begin to thunder up the Avenue Marceau from Les Halles, with the food and wine and petrol. But you can scarcely hear the traffic from my room in the Queen Elizabeth. And the telephone seldom rings.

Outside the streets are bright and brilliant, with hoardings and kiosks, with flowers on the street corners, with huge sleek cars moving away, chauffeur-driven from the Georges Cinq. You can discern French journalists in dark tight suits hurrying to the offices of *Paris-Match.* You can see model girls darting to the great houses, with very little on under their raincoats. But inside that hotel everything is very dark. Bedrooms are always dark in Paris; blinds are nearly always drawn. Thick muslin curtains block out reality. And Paul-Emile's and Ginette's apartment in Paris is even darker than the hotel. And here by 6 p.m. most evenings, when my day's work is done, I visit them.

The brightest room is the sitting-room and even this is heavy with shelves and shelves of good-taste books by good-taste people like Racine and Corneille. The hall is always lit by electric light. Floods of light and music and crowds of people dispel the gloom.

Fortunately (I feel) for Paul-Emile and Ginette the place is seldom empty. The sitting-room is constantly menaced by a mob of lively theatricals, all yelling and telling one another back-stage stories, shouting to each other in perpetual competition.

The bathroom is a reflection of the sitting-room at its wildest. Here, caught like flies in amber on the walls, are the signed photographs of the people you have just left shouting in the sitting-room.

The walls are wild with talent. Here are Lena Horne, smiling from ear to ear and saying 'Thank you' for something or other quite illegible. Satchmo. Danny Kaye. Carol (Baby Doll) Baker. Marlene. (At least four of Marlene, in swansdown cloak, in top hat and tails, Marlene bowing, Marlene in a group with Rubinstein.) Noël Coward carrying, nervously, a child. Claudette Colbert – two of her. Laurence Olivier. Maurice Chevalier. The eye cannot take them in, the faces, nor the heart admit the piercing messages of love, scrawled large in ball-point pen and flamboyant ink across the stomachs and bosoms of the stars.

Some of Ginette's Parisian friends are jealous of her star-spangled salon. They accuse her of going out of her way to catch the stars, as though she used a celestial shrimping net, mounted on a cloud somewhere in the Milky Way. But once a star has found its way to Ginette's apartment in the Avenue Marceau that star cannot live without that relaxation and intensity of enjoyment provided by Ginette's unique warmth of heart.

The great ones sit in Ginette's drawing-room, twinkling and greedy. Mostly, the moment they hit Paris they ring up. In answer to Ginette's invitation they 'Come on over' because they love it. They sit there, on Ginette's sofas and chairs, happily and fatly turning this way and that like chickens roasting on a spit in the window of a delicatessen, basking in the infra-red glow of Ginette's appreciation. They feel more themselves than they have ever felt. They become more witty. If they were charming, they are suddenly enchanting. In Ginette's presence they suddenly feel *real*. She is the perfect audience. As an audience, she is herself a star.

But this is not all of Ginette's character.

It is only the outside edge, the most obvious crust of her personality. Personality and character are two very different things, and many people who have one are deficient in the other. Ginette has both, to a degree of saturation. Hers is the loyalty, constantly tested by her show-biz friends, who don't tend to stay steadily and happily married to one another. Hers is the generosity, cheerfully tearing the dress from her back for someone who has fleetingly admired it. Courage, too, the two o'clock in the morning courage which dragged her and Paul-Emile through four years on the run, one jump ahead of the Nazis in Occupied France. Faith. Violence in love, violence in hate.

She hates antique shops, old rare furniture that is wobbly, tides. She loves soft ear-pillows, wide steel modern desks, hotels, luxury, Scotch on the rocks, fur.

It was Noël Coward who sent me to Ginette in the first place. He was sitting upon a chair by her bedside reading the galley proofs of the book *Why I'm Not a*

Millionaire, to which he was kind enough to write a fore-word. From time to time he laughed, which annoyed Ginette very much.

'It's Nancy Spain's new book,' he said, and when he heard that Ginette had never heard of me, added a short and wildly uncomplimentary character sketch. Undeterred, however, Ginette read the galleys, which were in a fearful tangle. She then wrote to me and asked what she should do with them. Startled, I replied: 'Dear Madame Seidmann, throw the bloody things away.' But the next time I was in Paris, taking photographs of the Duke and Duchess of Windsor's town house, I lunched with Ginette at the Avenue Marceau. And here began a friendship which means a very great deal to me.

I wouldn't like to count how many times I have been since, nor to list the pleasures to which Ginette has introduced me. There I heard 'Master' Coward tell her that, as a hostess, 'You exhibit all the more dashing characteristics of the water buffalo.' There Marlene played a record for me. 'I want to see the effect on you, sweetheart.' The record was put on the gramophone, Marlene crouched like a child on the floor. The Legs were folded under her. She crooned to the machine, which was apparently temperamental: 'Now, now, sweetheart, don't be that way. Be nice, now, sweetheart.'

Finally, the record started.

It was an L.P., thirty solid minutes of it at thirty-three and one-third revolutions per minute. It was applause. Hands clapping. Solid hand-clapping. Nothing else.

Every now and then Marlene would explain one of the finer points.

'That's me taking a bow,' she would say. Or, 'There I am, coming on again.'

It was her applause from a tour of Germany.

When the record came to an end I am afraid I became somewhat firm.

'Marlene,' I said, briskly, 'it's a quarter to three in the morning and you must go home. Come along now and I'll drive you back to your hotel.'

She put the record away, in a little cardboard suitcase of the kind that I used to take to school with an apple when I was very young. I dropped her at her hotel. She looked like a child of fifteen as she waved good night on the pavement and I turned the car round.

When I told this story to Lena Horne she said she saw Marlene's point of view. 'The applause will be very useful to her,' she said, without a smile, 'for piping into an album when she makes one.'

In Ginette's sitting-room I have seen all the great ones of show business, Judy Garland, Lynn Fontanne, Alfred Lunt, Chevalier, topping each other's stories.

Once indeed Lena and Noël Coward sat toe to toe, reminiscing about *another* party.

'Do you remember,' Lena asked her husband, Lennie Hayton, 'do you remember how great Noël was at that party?'

Lennie, I may say, had surpassed himself by bringing to Ginette's house his own little leather dry-martini kit, including the lemon, and was gravely mixing his own martinis.

'Sure,' said Lennie, glumly twisting a piece of lemon peel.

'But Lena was great, too; you were lovely, my darling; wasn't she lovely, Lennie, dear boy?' asked Noël.

'Sure,' said Lennie, rubbing a piece of lemon round the rim of the glass.

'And Lennie was lovely, too, weren't you, Lennie?' said Ginette, brushing by them.

'Sure,' said Lennie.

'But we keep on talking about ourselves all the time,' said Lena, graciously turning to Anton Dolin, who was sitting beside her. 'How is the Ballet?'

'Cut!' said Dolin, rising to leave.

I followed him to the stairs to say goodbye.

He told me he had seen me on TV the week before.

'You were good,' he said, 'but your teeth were terrible. Either don't smile so much or get them fixed.'

Halfway down the stairs to the lift he looked back at me.

'I'd like to be on *Juke Box Jury*,' he said. 'Could you fix that at the same time?'

Every Saturday at Marceau is much the same. A few people come in for drinks. The party gathers force. Someone goes to the piano. It gets later. Nine o'clock passes. Paul-Emile gets hungry. The whole brood, still giving an outsize performance, but by now broken up into its star component parts, wanders out 'on the town' . . .

Here, other Great Show Business Names join up, like mercury rushing back into itself when a thermometer tube is broken.

I love Ginette. I love Paul-Emile. I love their Saturday nights in Paris. Life led at this Marceau level is never boring, but it is inclined to tire. One must stay sober, as the nerves are on a constant jump, so as not to miss any brilliant remark. The ears strain, not to forget any words of any of the songs. Susan Fonda once suddenly sang:

> 'There's a telephone in my bosom
> And I'm calling right from my heart
> The Lawd is on the line . . .'

and I walked around in a dither for days until I met Susan again and made her write down the lyric for me. On this occasion we swapped impressions of the Marceau party where she had been singing, and we both agreed that our knowledge of humanity had been deepened and broadened and widened by the Seidmanns.

Ginette, possibly, lacks one quality. She has no critical faculty. (Paul-Emile is very critical indeed. Quite often his wit is biting.) Ginette accepts everyone on precisely the same level, without light or shade, undiscerningly, unhesitatingly. She accepts James Baldwin, Greta Garbo, the Profumos, Lady Diana Cooper, the racing crowd, exactly as they are. And she treats them all alike.

Ginette likes people to behave as they would like in their hearts to be. In her house they often give an intensified projection of themselves. She is delighted when they come unstuck and shout and screech and 'put one another on' and play the piano far into the night.

Paris is not a city where anyone normally keeps open house. It is a city of villages, closely connected, each village dedicated to a different way of life. And in the 16th and the 8th *arrondissements* the doors are usually tightly closed against intruders. Ginette holds the key to Right Bank Paris, that magic mile around the Georges Cinq and the Champs Élysées and the houses of couture where the air is scented and every other car is a Rolls-Royce.

In my heart I am a Left Bank girl. And when sometimes in July I would go to Paris to stay with Ginette I would often find myself sneaking across the river to Montparnasse.

One year, for example, Ginette introduced me to Frances Rich. Sculptress daughter of silent-movie star Irene Rich, she was also a friend of Katharine Hepburn's, so we had plenty to talk about. With her I went sketching in the Grande Chaumière where they do *croquis* (sketches) from 3 p.m. onwards.

As illuminating in its own way as Ginette's salon: that dusty little art class.

An old woman sits by the door. She takes two new francs entrance fee. She has a cardboard box lid, containing pieces of rubber and broken chalks and pencils for sale. Inside the classroom, which has a huge northern light, there is a rusty stove and endless wooden donkeys and broken chairs where the students prop their portfolios. It is exactly as it was in *Trilby's* day. It looks like a drawing by George Du Maurier. And there stands the model, on her throne.

Sometimes the model is a huge negress. Negresses are fascinating to draw, particularly when they are old, eyes heavily lidded, skin hanging in folds. Sometimes the model is a young girl, Bardot-type, who darts in, climbs out of her jeans and leather jacket and reveals a beautiful body that is a terrible bore. Sometimes the model is a real professional, an Englishwoman, old but still remarkable, with her hair dressed in combs, and beautiful, ballet dancer's feet.

The students are gathered all around the model, perched here and there like birds in an aviary.

There are young men with beards, playing at artists. They usually draw very badly. There are young girls in dirndl skirts and jangling bracelets. Here and there, old American ladies, tremblingly in search of their lost youth. And the Japanese, concentrated, scowling, often with real talent, drawing savagely and swiftly in black ink.

The first pose is held for half an hour. Then faster poses follow, of ten minutes each. Then the real excitement begins. Who can keep up with a pose of two minutes? A student must be pretty good to catch movement, life, pose, texture of skin, age, sex on paper in two minutes.

I have always loved drawing. The trouble is the way in which it absorbs me. After two hours of it I realise that I have lost the world and need a drink. And I reel out into the street again, relaxed as a kitten, seeing every street corner with new eyes.

I suppose since 1956 I must have spent about a week of every month in Paris – maybe more. Sometimes, when my work is over, I have time to play golf or to swim. At one time golf was the perfect release for me. I used to play eighteen holes in my imagination before I went to sleep at night, on some course well known to me. And I could seldom stay awake after the third hole.

I love the countryside of golf courses, the undulating meadows, fine woodlands, great oaks, cunning short holes amongst chestnut trees. I am never aware of the beauty of the landscape all around me as I lash the ball along the fairways or into the rough. Yet something of the green grass and the silence of the woods seeps into me, along with the lost balls in the undergrowth.

After a round of golf (assuming that my work has been done and all the cables have gone off) my idea of a complete day in Paris would be polished off by a quarter of an hour's swimming. My trouble is that I am inclined to work at everything I do. I work at golf, I even work at swimming, particularly when I am swimming in pools like the Paris piscines.

The Piscine Deligny, down by the Seine, the Piscine Molitor on the edge of the Bois: a life goes on there something like the life in the gymnasia of Ancient Rome. There is a snack bar and a restaurant. Young people pick each other up, and eat cherries and drink beer and spit the stones at each other, ignoring dedicated middle-aged pseudo-athletes like me.

I first learned to swim when I was about eight years old. Attached to a rope by a lady with very furry armpits I would be towed across the bath at speed, vainly trying to co-ordinate in time to the shouts of 'Won, two, Legs Together, *Three* . . .' This was the breast stroke.

Later, without anyone's help I acquired the trudgen stroke and the Australian crawl and became rather a fancy diver. I used (with fourpence in my pocket for the tram fare) to go off, with my bathing dress and rubber cap wrapped in a towel, to the Chillingham Road Baths, Newcastle upon Tyne. I walked both ways, as a matter of fact, spending my tram fares on a meat pie that I bought in a pie shop halfway. The taste of fourpenny meat pie, the gravy trickling down my chin, the tingle of the chlorine in my eyes, the heaviness with which I dragged my legs the last half-mile to my home, these things are a part of childhood happiness. Goodness, how I *worked* at swimming, imitating those gods and goddesses in the deep end, reading little paper-backed books, taking in lessons in diet and in training: deep breathing and the like.

Since then I have swum in many pools and lakes, in many seas. I have smashed my nose to smithereens, showing off in a shallow pool in Madeira. I have scraped my back, secretly sliding into the Lakes of Killarney in a heatwave. I have dived, with Sir Laurence Olivier, into the pool of Serena Dunn (she who married a Rothschild) and, I gather, outraged the butler because the bra of my bikini came adrift. I have swum endlessly, pleasurably, in the Mediterranean. I have even complained to myself of the rim of sun-tan oil and dirt along the edge of the shallow water in St. Tropez and Nice. But until I saw the turquoise depths of the Aegean behind the island of Skiathos I truly do not think that I knew what swimming *was* . . .

The pools, beautiful though they sometimes are, are no substitute for the real thing.

When I was an eight-year-old, funnily enough, I pre-ferred pools to the sea.

'Well,' I used to say, trying to explain my preference to some tiresome grown-up, 'they're nice and warm and tidy and you can dive into them.'

The only seas with which I had to compare the Chill-ingham Road Baths were, of course, the Irish Sea and the North Sea, which are both refined forms of torture, especially iced to stop the breath and the heart. When I think of the echoing, clamorous, claustrophobic Chill-ingham Road Baths and compare them (for example) with Carlos Thompson's and Lilli Palmer's pool near Zurich I have to admit that I am not really speaking of the same thing.

Lilli's pool is the most beautiful (I would say) in the world. It is on top of a mountain, surrounded by gardens and trees and hayfields; in the distance lies the panorama of the Jungfrau Mountains and Eiger and Monch. The pool itself, curiously curved like a semi-precious stone, can lie opaque and blue in a setting of dazzling snow.

But even in the Thompson pool, in the bright heat of the Swiss summer sun, I felt curiously enclosed. There was no spring released in my heart, no mad moment of joy as there was on the day when I forced my poor friend Roy Rutterford to drive me willy-nilly through North Africa to the Pillars of Hercules, so that I could swim in the Atlantic rollers, brilliant blue and fizzing green. And the Piscine Molitor cannot compare with the languid turquoise depths of the Aegean.

Pools are merely man-made tranquillisers designed to relax the muscles. They do not relax the tired muscle of the brain. For outside every pool there is a telephone. At the other end of the telephone there is every distraction the world has to offer: noise, excitement, people, people, stories, stories.

And the moment I pick up that receiver all the things I ever dreamed of accomplishing as I lay there, quietly ambitious, in the sun, are suddenly dissipated by the moment: the turning back into myself, the blind lust of finding out the truth.

In my island of Skiathos, washed on all its coasts by the Aegean Sea, there is no telephone. At least, I believe there is one in the police station. But you can only use it by appointment. And I have never tried.

LOVE ME, LOVE MY TELEPHONE CALL

The telephone is never an escape to anywhere. Even if you are in love, and relying upon a call from the beloved object to heave you out of a world where feet are heavy and clay-stuck: the telephone brings you right back upon yourself. From that double cuckoo ring I have never had anything but appointments broken, unnecessary intrusions – those exasperating people who ring and say, 'How are you?', and getting the reply 'Working', do not seem to have the sense to ring off. Letters are different. Letters are never anything but good news. And telephone calls that I originate myself often seem to work. But the incoming call is no escape whatsoever.

In my time, connoisseur that I am, I have sampled every means that imagination can offer of escape. Escape from tightened nerves, bouncing temper, sensation of exploding fireworks on the top of the skull. Why, there were nights when I worked for the *Daily Express* and faced a blank leader page, and would have to tailor a story to fill it, when the feeling that a razor was about to split me between sanity and madness became unbearable. On these nights, when the work was done, the nerves would refuse to go down: and the only way out then always seemed to be alcohol. Alcohol consumed in company with the colleagues in one or other of the pubs with which Fleet Street is lively.

After a TV show the same thing applies. I am usually in shows that demand 'the old spontaneous' expression. Unscripted, we are expected, in *Juke Box Jury* and *Any Questions* and *My Word!* and *It's My Opinion*, to provide entertainment for the public. As the bright white light shines in our eyes we write the script, verbally, filling the silence of the air with bright thought and happy anecdote.

Before the red studio light goes on, and the two notices 'Sound On', 'Vision On' stay steady, there is always thirty seconds' panic. A panic so extreme that I ask anyone who is around me, 'Why the hell do we do it?' The answer is always the same: 'The money.' And then we are on the air, and the adrenalin is rushing through the blood, and the terrors have disappeared under the impact of the cameras, the recognition of the audience, and the necessity of getting *them* to relax too. And after the performance one does not immediately feel drained dry. Those nerves stay up for hours after a performance.

I did an advertising series one year, all about Dentabs (tablets that clean teeth). Day after day the house rang to my proclamations: 'Ninety-nine out of a hundred children have decayed teeth – so probably have yours – but here comes something new to help. Dentabs. Tablets that clean teeth.'

The director took me on one side after a very twitchy display on 'Take One'.

'You're a nervy old thing, aren't you?' he said. 'Fancy that.'

Nervy. My goodness. I'll say so.

And when the show is over, and the nerves are tighter than the string of a kite, and nothing in this world will calm them down, this is the moment when one looks around wildly for the exit marked 'Escape'.

The movies, the theatre, the drink in the pub . . .

Because of the sudden absence of self-analysis and criticism, alcohol gives the illusion of escape. This is sheer nonsense. All it does is to provide an extra extension of energy (and nervous energy at that), leaving one even more exhausted in the morning. Drink banishes shyness. And I greatly enjoy the taste of drink. I love champagne and almost any white wine, as long as it is dry. But there is no escape there, not even drinking in company.

Being in love is, of course, the perfect escape. Requited love, more than any other, provides the perfect springboard to eternity. Take care, however, lovers, would-be lovers, that love does not then absorb the whole of your life and work and mop you up like blotting paper. Then stars and omens, symbols of luck, all turn upon the one thing: the personality of the beloved.

In our childhood my sister and I used interminably to consult *Napoleon's Book of Fate*. There was a great series of questions and answers. One would pick the right answer by slamming down a pin over a series of zodiac signs. Then one would turn the page and the answer to the question would spring up. I remember my sister's sheer horror the day she asked, 'What is my beloved doing at this moment?', and she got the reply, 'At Fisticuffs with his Landlord.' Believe it or not at tea-time in he walked with a black eye.

Take care of requited love: watch out, or you will be back home again, walking in at the door marked 'Entrance'. The loved one, black eyes and all, becomes a part of life, 'for real', something to be taken seriously, reacted to and pondered over. 'Is your relationship good or bad?' we suddenly ask. 'Are we making anyone else unhappy?' 'Shall we live together for ever more?' These questions are never even asked of love, true love. The answers are there long before the questions are framed.

I sat once with John Betjeman the poet, and we talked of love.

'I am always in love,' he remarked, dreamily. 'It is delirious. Delicious. I cannot remember a day going by when I have not been in love with someone or something. It is the mainspring of life, the meaning of all existence.'

To be in love is to escape into something, a boundless, limitless world in which there are suddenly endless possibilities of growth and development. Innermost thoughts, forgotten ambitions, most sacred secret dreams, all that you have ever hoped to be since the age of two suddenly surges up again, like magic.

And with what passion do I love. I love indeed. Since childhood I can remember becoming obsessed by London, Paris, New York, Chicago, many ships, some horses, Manchester, a few people, Liverpool, a great many ideas, a recording of 'The Surrey with the Fringe on Top' and Beethoven's Fifth Symphony. I have had long and lasting love affairs with a newspaper, Noël Coward's autobiography *Present Indicative*, Emlyn Williams' memoir *George* and one or two musical shows like *Oklahoma!* and *Annie Get Your Gun*.

I have been in love with Fellini's *La Dolce Vita* (saw it

five times), *Destry Rides Again* (ditto), Gingold's various satirical revues, caviar, vodka, *La Belle et La Bête*, *Les Enfants du Paradis*, oysters, and that maddening tune from *Never on Sunday*.

Each of these obsessions have acted upon me as a springboard to eternity: each has shown me the possibilities that life can offer. Escape, in my opinion, is not a matter of escaping from something. It is an escape into something – something that approximates temporarily to the absolute good.

At the moment then, when I became so obsessed by the Greek island of Skiathos, I suppose that in my heart I was approaching the end of my love affair with the charted, civilised Europe, the Europe of Michelin and the three-star hotels, the Europe I thought I understood. I was already sick of my relationship with Paris and was about to use her as a jumping-off place, a gateway to the unknown.

Chapter Six

Round the World between Two *My Words!*

What sauce, you will say, to speak of Paris as a jumping-off place. But there is no disrespect in the phrase. Everything begins in Paris. Most honeymoons. Nearly all my own personal adventures. For example, it was in Paris that comedian Jimmy Edwards and I planned a day's hunting, an insane adventure, dominated for days by my shopping list, which remarked between 'Baked Beans' and 'Repair the gutter on the roof' somewhat startlingly 'Get Horse'. It was in Paris that I really got to know Marlene, Joan Plowright and Sir Laurence Olivier. And this was before Sir Laurence had made Joanie Lady Olivier and before they had become mother and father of two zonkingly beautiful children. And it was from Paris, obviously, that I flew round the world with Air France, between two editions of *My Word!*, and demanded forty-eight hours' stop-off time to break my journey in Athens and so see my island.

For since the encounter at my doctor's table, when Mrs Rena Harper obligingly suggested that she could buy some land for me, I had become madly in love with the home movies she had shown me of a green island, with golden beaches where turquoise sea lay like silk.

Rena Harper, Greek, born in Athens, married to an Englishman called Kenneth Harper, is full of go and vim and vigour. I like her very much. She has auburn hair, a tawny skin, unusual goodly eyes and she is great fun to be with. In the time following our first meeting, at my doctor's dinner-table, I would often accept Rena's hospitality, drinking ouzo and eating pistachio nuts, while, bemused, I studied maps of the island, tried to reckon up the cost of a journey to Athens and the cost of a caique to convey myself and my car across from Orei or Pifki, the cost of an hotel room while the house was being built: most important of all the house itself. Plans, how much would an architect cost? How could one get the land flat enough to build on? Was the land on the north of the island as good as the land to the south-east? And so on . . . and so forth . . .

All these subjects were of a heady fascination to me. Evening after evening I sat in Rena's comfortable chairs and ate her splendid food and discussed, discussed, discussed. We were both filled with enthusiasm for the project. And then all at once the opportunity came. I was about to see the island.

Symbolic perhaps, the first inkling I had of a trip round the world came the night my father died. He died in October and it was some time before my shocked recognition of the fact that he was actually mortal, and not immortal as I had always believed. After the funeral my life was crowded with responsibilities of one sort or another, for although my heart seemed to have forgotten its function, I still had dates to fulfil, columns to write, appearances to make. You might think that a public life is a fearful thing to someone at a time of grief. In fact, it is not. It acts as a sort of harness, the kind of harness that holds a horse steady between the shafts long after life has gone from the animal, and with impetus from the mild cart behind it, keeps it trotting steadily upon its way . . .

So it wasn't until the February of the year following my father's funeral that Stafford Somerfield, Editor of the *News of the World*, kind, imaginative, with his 22-carat heart and a speaking voice that would do a great actor credit, persuaded me to go and discuss a round-the-world trip with Air France.

'But I've only *got* ten days,' I moaned, eager to stay in my tiny rut, trotting in my little harness. 'Do you really think I can do justice to Bangkok and Hong Kong and Tokyo and places like that with a day in each?'

'I don't know,' said Staffy. 'Just you go and discuss it with Cyril McGhee and Jack Bamford.'

I transferred myself to the Air France office, where I discussed everything with Jack Bamford and Cyril McGhee. Cyril, a pleasant Scot, with a scarred face that gives him a dashingly rakish air, hair striped with silver like a badger, seemed unperturbed at the time that I offered him, ten days between two *My Words!* . . . 'Why not?' he asked, mildly, pulling polar routes and time-tables towards him. 'Round the world in ten days. It's rather a good story I think.'

And then I heard myself saying something truly astonishing.

'Can Granny come too?' I was asking.

Cyril still seemed unperturbed.

'Who is Granny?' he wanted to know.

The words falling over one another as I tried to explain, I blocked Cyril in on the subject of 'Granny', Elizabeth Beatrice Mary Werner Laurie, mother of Jonnie, enthusiastic Women's Institute member, widow of T. Werner Laurie, publisher extraordinary.

'She will stop me making a fool of myself,' I explained. 'You see, I am a sort of chameleon. I take colour from my surroundings so quickly. When I am in America I get American so quickly that nobody at home can understand my copy after a bit. I am a hopeless romantic. Granny is a realist. Granny has her feet on the ground. Granny is super.'

Cyril began to laugh.

'All right,' he said. 'Granny can come too. Have you broken the news to her?'

This rocked me back a bit.

'No,' I said. And I went home, to the little house in South Kensington where I then lived, and said to Granny (who was staying with us) somewhat self-consciously, 'How'd you like to come round the world with me?'

Granny's mouth scarcely fell open. I have no idea if

she thought I was joking. Anyway, she didn't even pause.

'Very much,' said she.

Granny, you see, is a bright spark indeed. I've no idea how old she is, and I don't think it matters anyway. She is charming, tough as they come, and there is nothing she likes better than a sing-song at the old songs of World War I, sitting round a piano with kindred spirits, and a gin and tonic in one hand. She has soft white hair, sharp eyes that miss very little, and when she is not living in a seventeenth-century cottage in Loxwood, Sussex, with a huge brown poodle called Ambar, she loves to travel. She is always whirling to relatives in America and Canada, or off across Europe in a coach with the Women's Institute, and heaven knows (I thought) if she can do *that*, ten days round the world will be quite a cake-walk for her . . .

She is great company. She loves people. She gets huge pleasure from anything well done, and as long as she is left alone and not messed about with interpreters she has the gift of instant communication. In Austria, in Germany, in Holland, she will battle away without one word of the language and return to the hotel, laughing, and triumphant, with the goods she set out to buy. No floor-walker who has ever met Granny in a wild shopping mood will ever forget her. And, on top of all this, she is a diabetic, with her diabetes lightly worn, like a gay spring hat. Believe me, Granny has such *panache* that she makes you feel that 'having diabetes' is the only thing. Not only desirable, but fashionable.

I spent a jolly four days going round the embassies and

the legations collecting visas for the two of us. The Thai Embassy was the smallest. There was only one perfectly splendid girl typing away there, with a huge pile of passports in front of her. In the end I got Visa No. 630/2505, 'good for a single journey to Thailand, valid for sixty days' with a superb rubber stamp showing some sort of Siamese eagle, with a hat on and wild wings, crouching nervously at the top of the page. The Japanese Embassy was the biggest. In incredible splendour, mainly consisting of heavy panels and oak beams, I collected Visa No. 19032, with a squirt of Japanese characters at the top and the signature of S. Kehio. This was good for 'Multiple Journeys to Japan for *Business*' and I could stay 180 days if I liked. What a fraud I felt, the passport in my hand. I was going to stay in Bangkok forty-eight hours and in Tokyo three days. What delirious madness.

I returned her passport to Granny, explaining that we would have to start our great adventure from Paris. Curiously enough, Granny looked quite pleased.

'And you do realise,' I explained, 'that we are going to see my island? Skiathos? You don't mind . . . I mean, that is really, deep down, why I am going on this trip . . . It may be very uncomfortable, Granny. . .'

'You try and stop me,' said she.

I rang up Rena Harper and explained the master plan. We synchronised watches, as it were. She and Kenneth would already be in Athens and with typical Harper kindness they would meet us at the airport and we would all drive to the island in a Cadillac provided by Air France. It would mean leaving Athens early in the morning. Maps lay all over my desk. Timetables lay all over Cyril McGhee's. I have no idea what Granny felt like, but I heard her murmuring something about 'What clothes shall I take?' Poor Granny. She had picked the wrong audience there. I have never (but never) been able to advise anyone about clothes. Looking at my maps I muttered something about it being hot in the East. After Paris (I thought) everything would be hot. Paris (I was pretty sure) would be cold.

'You must get vaccinated, Granny,' I said. 'You must get vaccinated for yellow fever, black-water fever, small-pox and everything. They won't let us into the USA without a vaccination certificate . . .'

'We're going to the USA?' asked Granny, reasonably bewildered.

I pointed to the map.

'We fly back by Anchorage in Alaska,' I explained, 'and we get off there for breakfast. And technically that is an entry to America. But actually we ought to get vaccinated because of the water in Thailand and in Iran and all that . . .'

'We're going to Iran?' asked Granny, who had once travelled to America with a Persian lady in the same cabin, longed to see her again and thought she ought to warn her of her approach.

'Well,' I said, looking at my maps and timetables, 'we only stop there for refuelling, and in the middle of the night. But perhaps she could come to the airport. It's

Persia, really, isn't it?' I asked Granny. 'You know the *Rubáiyát of Omar Khayyám* and all that bit?'

Granny didn't know, and neither did I. We had never imagined it. It was all simply a map to us at that point and there was little we could do to visualise anything. We were vaccinated. We 'took' alarmingly and for some days reeled under the combined impact of black-water fever, yellow fever, bubonic plague and smallpox. I finished one series of *My Word!* Then, convalescent, with Cyril McGhee we flew to Paris. Paris, which for Granny was a jumping-off place for Athens, Bangkok, Hong Kong and Tokyo. Paris, which for me, saucy though it seems, was a jumping-off place for the deeply imagined island of Skiathos.

IN GREEK 'MY WORD!' IS A FOUR-LETTER WORD

The radio quiz game *My Word!* is now almost better known outside England than it is at home.

Sent out by the BBC's transcription service on offer to the English-speaking radio stations of the world, it is bought with enthusiasm and played by addicted stations in Australia, Hong Kong, New Zealand, Cincinnati, North and South Carolina, Jamaica, Canada, Barbados, New York (on the F.M. radio), South Africa and India.

Because of the personalities of the people in the show ('You all sound as if you were having such a good time,' said a station director to me once in Cincinnati) the programme has an obsessive, drug-like quality about it.

Once you are hooked you cannot leave *My Word!* alone. I know of station technicians who wait trembling to tear the packaging of the new series, who play them back to listen to certain contributions. I know Claudette Colbert in Barbados comes in from the warm blue sea. And I have had letters from people in New Zealand who take their transistor radios along with them on picnics rather than miss a syllable from Frank Muir and Denis Norden, the two male participants. Wherever I go people ask me the history of the show, wherever I go they ask what are Frank and Denis *like?*

Well, I first met *My Word!* about eight years ago on a freezing cold night in the Aeolian Hall in Bond Street, London.

We had one of those damnable trial runs. The team on this occasion consisted of Frank Muir, Denis Norden, Lady Barnett, myself and John Arlott, poet and cricket commentator. The *Miss SHE* fashion contest finals were held the same night in the Albert Hall, so I was lashed into the fullest of evening dress and felt an absolute ass, teetering about in my tiara in broad daylight.

Dazed, I sat on a little gold chair on the draughty stage of the Aeolian Hall. Round One. What is an ethiolata? What a polypod? Round Two, before I had scarcely recovered, wincing, from this dastardly assault on my vocabulary, Complete the Following Quotation . . . or *worse* give the lines before 'Far brighter than this gaudy melon flower.'

Then, it seemed to me some hours later, we were

113

asked to identify a quotation and the boys launched themselves into fantasy stories, showing how the quotation, famous saying, or phrase originated. Upon this astonishing last round the future of *My Word!* depended. In this round Frank and Denis (who for many years had blushed unseen, writing brilliant material for Jimmy Edwards, Peter Sellers and others) suddenly emerged in all their glory as fully fledged comedians. In this round they can indulge their love of puns, their verbal dexterity, their humours to the full. I once sat at a table with Sir Laurence Olivier and a TV producer who was about to produce Olivier in *John Gabriel Borkman* and watched Larry forced to listen to the producer's reproduction of Frank Muir's tale as to how the phrase 'There's Many a Slip Twixt the Cup and the Lip' originated. The producer was an addict. Sir Laurence was not, anyway at that time. And he seemed pretty stunned at the idea of 'Manet asleep twixt the carp and the leap' in the Bois de Boulogne.

On that first evening in the Aeolian Hall I felt very like Sir Laurence. Frank said that a polypod was a laxative for a parrot. Denis said that when Jane Russell met Sabrina in the corridor of a train one said to the other, 'Shall we open a second front now?' Lady Barnett and I sat there, stunned.

Then the game lapsed into silence for a year. And then we plunged into a full and desperate *My Word!* life, presenting it all over the Midlands.

As it was the invention of two wide boys from

Birmingham, Tony Shryane and Edward J. Mason, we had to pin the programme down in the Birmingham area. And we travelled wildly through Warwickshire and Worcestershire like a tiny circus troupe. Each week we would set out, meeting on platforms in St. Pancras and Euston, travel to some farther and farther-flung place, perform before some startled audience in Ashby de la Zouch, or Great Yarmouth or Middlesbrough or North-ampton, Oxford, Cambridge or Banbury. And then we would catch the last train back to London. Or lie, rigid, twitching, cold and sleepless, in some unfamiliar provincial hotel before we caught the milk train back to London.

Tony Shryane, the producer of *My Word!*, is a bright, exceedingly intelligent man with a strong nose and a streak of ruthlessness that allows him to 'tape' one hour and then cut out enough to leave one half-hour's pro-gramme. With him, holding the scissors, as you might say, is Valerie Hodgetts, his secretary and production assistant, who keeps the score, handles the bookings and often rings me up on the morning to remind me where I should be performing that night.

Edward J. Mason, who produces the questions week by week (and also a script of *The Archers*, an agricultural soap opera, day by day), is a big man with a beard and a curious resemblance to William Shakespeare. Ted plays golf with one club, a rusty old cleek with a hickory shaft, and he met his wife Rene when they were both work-ing in Cadbury's chocolate factory. Ted swears he ran a trolley into her, covered with Milk Tray chocolates. Tony and Ted, writing the programme, editing it, booking it, flinging it out in car-load lots to Overseas, Transcription and the Home Service of the BBC, control our destinies.

'We' are the team. One half of us consists of the Boys, Frank Muir and Denis Norden, famous script-writing team who grew to manhood with the daddy of all the script writers, Ted Kavanagh, who was responsible for *It's that Man Again* and Tommy Handley in World War II. The Boys became famous in their own right, and picked up award after award, for their material for Jimmy Edwards, their series *Take It From Here*, *Whack-O!* and *The Seven Faces of Jim*.

They are both tall and well groomed, dandified and exquisite as a couple of giraffes. They are an American's idea of all that an Englishman should be. Frank is six foot six, and he wears a little curling soft moustache like an officer in the Brigade of Guards in an old novel by Ouida. Frank is very country squire indeed, and his home is littered with guns, cameras, fishing rods, lawn-mowers and other hobbies taken up, absorbed and laid aside. Denis is more citified, sheltering behind a pair of heavy horn-rimmed spectacles, nervously tapping a cigarette between anxious fingers, doodling endless, somewhat psychopathic, doodles. Both boys have indecent sex appeal. Both are married. Both have two children. Both are members of the Savile Club, like our chairman Jack Longland, who succeeded John Arlott in the furious business of controlling the team.

Jack Longland is an athlete. He was an Olympic pole-vaulter, he nearly conquered Everest in the 1930s, he is the Director of Education for Derbyshire. Because he has to control the team, he lurks, smoking a small pipe, behind a pretended schoolmasterliness.

And then, where we once had the restlessly brilliant novelist, the late E. Arnot Robertson, there is now the placidly brilliant Dilys Powell. Dilys is married to Leonard Russell of the *Sunday Times* and when I acquired my title deeds for Skiathos she angelically translated them and painstakingly taught me my Greek vocabulary. Dilys has now replaced Arnot, and there is no gap in the programme at all. But I should not allow this page to turn without paying Arnot a tribute. I was very fond of her. She was a gifted, whole-hearted, fascinating creature and she left us all shaken when she died so untimely.

On our various wild trips Arnot had revealed herself as a 'secret bun-eater'. She would sit, happily munching Bath buns in the buffet, while Denis and Frank and I called for stronger things. She would bring picnic baskets, full of buns, to the shows, often ringing up on the morning to remind me where to be, and to ask did I want tea or coffee in the Thermoses?

All through the first years of *My Word!* I was under considerable pressure because of my work for the *Daily Express*. And I used to insist on dashing back to London after the show. So *My Word!* became for me an oasis indeed, an escape hatch in the middle of the week, away from the real world and its pressures, a wild night out with the Boys. Idiotic adventures would consume us. Railway carriages would empty as we boarded them. Racing up platforms, leaping, with seconds to spare, into the relevant railway carriage, stranded in stub-laden waiting-rooms in Manchester, waiting for the night train to amble in at 1.30 a.m. from Birkenhead, Frank and I would huddle in our duffel coats. Or we would nod off, upright and aching, beside a sozzled soldier in full kit. Or we would knock up terrible hotels and demand food, drinking brandy from tooth-glasses. The evenings were curiously like my war years: uncomfortable, extraordinary and filled with dotty comradeship. Pushing Edward J. Mason out of our sleeping compartments just as the train was leaving, listening to Denis's macabre description of his early-morning tea clanking towards him along the tar-macadamised road at Ashby de la Zouch (he swore it was the only connecting link between his bedroom and the kitchen), seeing Frank who cannot pronounce his 'r's get served with a 'warm spoon' instead of an aspirin . . . all this was absolute drivel, but it cemented our show, which now goes round the world.

Then there were the audiences. In its early stages *My Word!* travelled to find them, to hospitals, factories, civic centres. We would stand in mayors' parlours discussing mayoral chains or in hospital administrative offices, while matrons tried to feed us, drinking warm gin and tonic and gulping down sandwiches and sausage rolls and little mauve cakes with crystallised violets on them. We would hire cars to get home, allowing Frank to drive us. Then

Denis and I would sing, most horribly, both knowing every single word of every popular song that has ever been written. Or we would hire cars with chauffeurs to drive us, and the chauffeur would regale us with terrible stories of life in the Royal Mews. But now *My Word!* is an established thing and the audiences come to us, to the various studios of the BBC in London, to the Playhouse Theatre, to Piccadilly One (which is haunted) or to the Aeolian Hall.

We meet, usually at 7 p.m., and try to drown our nerves and fears in the nearest pub. Then we try to get a look at the questions, and Edward J. Mason won't let us. He and Jack Longland go off into a corner with a huge portmanteau filled with dictionaries and swot up their answers, while Dilys and Frank and Denis and I pretend we don't care. We cross the road to the studio, feeling very far from 'spontaneous' . . . and then the game hits us, precisely like one of those Atlantic rollers that can break your leg if you don't know how to swim.

I must admit that *My Word!* is a joyous holiday for me. I never think of it as work at all. If I did it would hang over me all the week, intimidating and terrifying. But simply because it is sandwiched between writing a column for *News of the World* and a column for *She* and all the other bits and pieces of my life, more often than not I bob along on *My Word!* as on the crest of a wave.

Chapter Seven

I Have a Word for the Greeks

It was a wild and blusterous day in February when Granny and I arrived in Paris after a session of *My Word!*, and then broke our world-circling journey with an evening at a celebrated restaurant called Les Assassins. It was very cold. Frost sharpened up the pavements and cooled the sleet that battered at our faces. Granny and I had been promised a sing-song at Les Assassins to warm us up.

'We will eat black pudding and cassoulet,' said François Girard, the area sales and public relations representative of Air France. 'Les Assassins is seventh heaven for me. I used to go there in my student days.'

Since Girard was a charming, good-looking man from Normandy with a big soft moustache and a beautifully modulated voice, something like Charles Boyer's, we were inclined to hang upon his every word. Granny thought she was in for something like a Loxwood-type sing-song with renderings of 'Who were you with, last night?' and 'Hullo, hullo, who's your lady friend?' and 'If you were the only girl in the world'. My mind was open.

'Is there anyone else in Paris you would like to bring along as well?' Cyril McGhee enquired. So after some thought Granny and I invited Claud Wittelson (who makes all the fur coats for Balmain and Balenciaga), Lina (one of the Balmain mannequins) and Ginette. Claud and Ginette seemed startled when they heard we were going to Les Assassins. And after I had had a good chance to look around, when we had actually arrived there, I could see why.

Picture if you can a restaurant on two floors, lighted dimly by guttering candlelight, with red-checked table-cloths, very hot. Enormously overfull and crowded, with many people singing and swaying in time to their singing, drumming on the table with black-handled two-pronged forks and steel knives. Every now and then one of their number, as if the spirit moved him, as at a prayer meeting, would leap to his feet and sing or shout an interminable song (many verses, even more choruses) amid shouts and, indeed, screeches of laughter. The food and drink, which arrived very swiftly indeed, were plentiful and (as Granny so rightly said) 'very different from West Sussex'. Granny beamed. She loved it all. She would have been happier, she confided to me, in a low, confidential tone, if she had known a *few* of the songs: words and music.

'I wonder if you *would* be happier, Granny darling,' I replied, 'because judging from the look of disapproval on Claud Wittelson's face all these songs are very rude.'

The songs spread sideways and gathered us in and

swept all before them. Girard was now on his feet, singing wildly, and sweeping the room along in paroxysms
of delight. Lina, the mannequin, was lifted suddenly in
the air by a gentleman from the next table, and everyone
drank her health. 'These songs are as dirty as a stuffed-up
drain,' said Ginette. '*I* should not be here . . . let alone
Granny.'

'Disgraceful,' said Claud Wittelson.

Granny beamed.

Even with *my* imperfect knowledge of French I had
a rough idea that we were now being brought into the
songs, our ancestors, the Queen and most of the Royal
Family. Gulping down my cassoulet, I told Granny as
much as I could understand.

'What a pity,' she said. 'Perhaps we shouldn't stay
if they are going to sing things like that about the
Queen . . .'

So we sneaked back to our hotel, Granny still beaming,
and in the morning, in the first of a series of luxurious
Air France jets, we flew to Rome.

Believe me, I am a connoisseur of airlines. I know
the difference between one aeroplane and another. And
you cannot get better treatment in the world than by
Air France. Every time you step into a Caravelle or an
Air France Boeing you step into the rarefied atmosphere
of Right Bank Paris, scented, exquisitely Parisian, with
champagne and caviar, with magnificent food served
as in some mildly religious ritual. You simply cannot
compare a long-distance Air France jet with any other.

For example, my very first flight was to Dublin, in 1945. I flew to do research on Mrs Beeton, to travel round the lakes of Killarney in her footsteps, making notes where she had kept a diary. I was terribly sick, buffeted all the way, and reeled from the plane in Dublin more dead than alive. I have flown with airlines in America, hopping from one town 'in the sticks' to another, in planes that flew no higher than the pigeons. And once in Claudette Colbert's private plane I flew to Palm Springs from Los Angeles unpressurised, with the most terrible resultant earache. I have flown to Liverpool and seen wheels fall off. I have watched engines cut out, and propellers slowly grind to a stop in mid-air. So when I say that I felt homesick for the Air France plane you will know that this is not idle praise. It is carefully thought-out one-upmanship to travel Air France, sinfully sybarite.

Beaming beside me on our flight to Rome, Granny helped herself to roast suckling pig, champagne, chocolate profiteroles.

'Granny, do you think you should?' I asked her mildly. 'What about your diabetes?'

'The hell with it,' said Granny smartly. 'I'll take two pills instead of one . . .'

And this, bless her brave heart, was Granny's attitude throughout the next ten days as we reeled, at six hundred miles an hour, from Paris to Rome, from Rome to Athens, from Athens to Bangkok, Bangkok to Tokyo, Tokyo to Alaska and home.

In Athens it was freezing. Granny had not been

prepared for this. I had told her that Athens was hot, and she had left all her warm clothes behind her in Paris. There at the airport were Rena and Kenneth Harper and Mr Drakopoulos, a very cuddly Greek gentleman indeed, who gave the impression that his arms were full of flowers which he was about to lay at our feet. Granny and I loved him. He accompanied us to the Grande Bretagne, we settled into our rooms. Rena told us she would call for us to take us out to dinner, and that we would start for the island the next morning at about 4 a.m.

'Do you mind?' I asked Granny. 'We probably shan't get to bed until about two a.m.?'

'I don't mind anything,' said Granny.

There was a nightmare quality to that evening. Rena had a great many friends, all Greek, who could speak French. We sat around in the drawing-room of their house, communicating like mad. Granny, with only English at her command, started to wilt a little. By about 10 p.m. we arrived at the restaurant. Almost at once musicians appeared and started to play the tune from *Never on Sunday* in Granny's right ear. We drank ouzo. We drank yellow wine with resin in. I talked excitedly in French and English about my island. Granny, manfully, bolted ouzo, made a face, bolted retsina, made another face, accepted (gratefully) a gin and tonic, and then saw with a little start of surprise that she was expected to eat a baby octopus. Whenever she caught my eye she beamed.

And, believe it or not, when a tiny crescent moon

hung low over the Parthenon next morning at 4 a.m., Granny, rubbing her two hours' sleep from her eyes, somehow managed a half-beam. (What a heroine! There should be a special medal struck for *anyone* who goes round the world with N. Spain, let alone a diabetic in her late sixties . . .)

We stood on the pavement with Kenneth Harper and Rena Harper in the dawn. We were all rather silent and sleepy, but Rena and I, as usual, were fired with enthusiasm and excitement which kept us both very energetic. To begin with we were all very good-tempered.

We met our driver. Brown face, wrinkled neck, features that looked as though they had been carved from wood, he wore a broad-brimmed black hat, a mourning armband, and somehow achieved the strange effect of a tortoise modelling an advertisement for Sandeman's port. He spoke fast Greek to Rena, and a few halting, very polite, English words to us. After an interminable chat we loaded everything in the boot, clambered into the car and drove off. Hesitantly (or so it seemed to me) the sun rose. In the back of the car I now became aware of another silent passenger. 'Your engineer,' said Rena, shortly.

We went pouring along the main road out of Athens towards Salonika. To begin with, the road was good. Metalled and true, it flew along, bright with advertisements, dotted with shrines, grey-green with olive groves. The sun was scarcely hot. Like a huge golden coin, it shone over my right shoulder, rising over Athens. We sped along to Thebes, turned right and crossed by a bridge at a town called Kalkis on to the island of Euboia that lies between the Greek mainland and the Sporades, where *my* island Skiathos is.

'We should take the ferry from Atlanta to Aedipsos,' said Rena rapidly. 'But I'm not at all sure if the ferry is running as early as this in the morning, and since you can only have so short a time, we are going to travel through Euboia on the mountain road.'

'Good, Rena,' said Granny, and patted her on the back.

'Quite right, Rena,' I said, jerking about in the front. 'Anyway, Euboia is very interesting, I'm sure. Isn't it where the centaurs come from? Perhaps we will meet one . . .'

'Nobody in Greece knows what time the ferry goes, at any time of year, anyway,' said Kenneth mildly.

And then the woody, rocky, precipitous horrors of the mountain road through Euboia closed around us. We wormed our way through dense forest, over a road that was more like a track, where puddles lay, and fallen leaves drifted from a sad and soggy winter. We broke cat ice in the ruts of the track as we squelched through, at about fifteen miles an hour. Low branches whacked the roof of the Cadillac. Brambles seemed to twine themselves in our way like something from a fairy tale. As the hours groaned by, in time to the creaking of our springs, and we had not breakfasted, I started to get worried about Granny's diabetes. Granny didn't. She just beamed.

Finally we stopped the car in an apology for a village and bought grey, flinty bread from a tumbledown bakery. Hens ran by, with thin necks and feathers sticking out. Fascinated women with black wool stockings wound around their heads peered at us through the windows of the car. Poor Granny, who had a little ulcer on her gum, reeled back from the bread in horror. 'Nonsense,' I said, cruelly, stuffing it into her mouth. 'We don't want you in a coma, now, do we, Granny?' Granny roared with laughter, and suddenly recollected all the little bottles of liqueur which Air France had lavished upon us, from Paris to Rome, from Rome to Athens. Framboise, green chartreuse, brandy, Grand Marnier: they lay there in Granny's handbag and saved our lives. Even the engineer woke up and drank some Grand Marnier. But he still scowled.

Jerking about in the front of that hellish Cadillac, as the fiery fumes of framboise and green chartreuse burned a sizeable hole in my stomach, I laid my aching head against the window and laughed weakly, contrasting the true Greece, the Greece that was still sliding by the windows, with that Greece of which I had dreamed. Chewing on the grey bread, gulping the intoxication of the chartreuse, I heard Granny mutter, 'I have a word for the Greeks.'

'Have you, then?' I whispered delicately back. 'I think you'd best not say it.'

'Fine people,' said the driver, suddenly in Greek. 'Fine country.'

And he waved, in a very hammy way, around him at two or three ladies also looking very like tortoises, spinning from distaffs, walking slowly along amongst the undergrowth. There were mules, too, which bucketed off into the ditch when we approached. They wore wooden saddles, rakishly loaded down with green boughs, and they looked lean and hopeless, with bones that stuck out.

Finally, when the whole thing had become insupportable, the woods were suddenly behind us, the sun suddenly shone warmly on our backs. And there, ahead of us through some pine trees, there was the sea.

The sea did not let us down. Blue, silver, turquoise, green, sighing gently along a sandy beach, it looked exactly as it had in all Rena's home movies. Beautiful. Shining. The sea at least was a dream come true. And we hurled ourselves from the car, like whoever it was in the Greek Army, calling out: 'Thalassa! Thalassa!'

Chapter Eight

The Pifki-Hilton

It was warm. The sun between my shoulder blades actually created a hot patch. For five minutes, at all events, Granny was properly dressed. In her linen coat, mauve as a crocus, she went skipping down the road towards the sand, towards the pine trees. The driver remained in the Cadillac. Deprived of our weight, it began, mole-like, to dig its way into the sand. It burrowed wildly. The driver had obviously never encountered this phenomenon before. Both Kenneth Harper and I were as obviously used to it. As one we leapt on to the bumper and with our weight held the one non-spinning rear wheel securely on what remained of the road. Grinning contentedly, the driver drove, flinging us off like flies. Kenneth and I landed (bruised) on all fours. I felt like telling him that Granny had a word for the Greeks . . .

This, Kenneth explained, was Pifki. Here was the rendezvous for the caiques. And there, patiently bobbing at anchor, a caique and rather a nice-looking sailing yacht were waiting. No rowing boat, however. Unless we cared to swim out to the caiques we still had a bit of time on our hands while we waited for the dinghy, to sit on the sand in the sun.

Under pine trees, by the water's edge, there was a thatched hut that in those days passed muster as a 'restaurant'. The Greeks build and rebuild so quickly that as I write this for all I know the Pifki-Hilton may be standing there, thirteen storeys high. Rena, looking very pretty and pleased with it all, said she had ordered eggs and coffee. But Granny knew better.

'Those Greeks,' she said. 'I have been in there to see. They have put two eggs into a gallon-sized fish-kettle of cold water. It'll take all day to boil . . .'

So, eggless and coffee-less, gallant Granny clambered into the dinghy and was rowed to the caique. By and by we all climbed on board. Granny and Rena and Kenneth disappeared into a cabin, aft of the mast. But I found a kitchen chair in the stern, and there in the sun I fell asleep. I dreamed I was riding a horse, so I suppose it must have been pretty rough. Anyway, four hours later I was awakened by Rena, tugging at my sleeve, laughing, calling out, all at once. Pointing across a mile of tumbling green and blue and white surf she showed me an island, green as an emerald, rising from the sea.

'Look! Look!' she cried. 'There beyond that little lighthouse. . .'

I saw a tiny island, now nearer than the main island. Sure enough, perched on it there was a light. Behind it were cliffs, green cliffs, where the sea dashed perpetually.

132

'That is your land,' she said, more soberly. 'That is your land.'

A 'PLOT' IS A LOT OF LEGAL DEEDS ENTIRELY SUR-ROUNDED BY DRACHMAI

My land. That I should own a piece of a Greek island. The thing is a fantasy. How on earth had I done it?

Well, all those months ago, when Rena and I had first met at my doctor's dinner-table, I didn't really believe in it at all. But then some months later Norman, my doctor, rang, and said the thing was done. Rena had bought the land for me and it would cost about £100.

Later, over the maps and the movies, I had explained to Rena that I was indeed taking the whole thing very seriously and I wanted my land, but I wanted a *good* bit. It must face south-east, so that I had the morning sun, and it must have a beach *and* run sheer down into the sea, so that I had deep bathing and beach bathing for the children. Rena was most obliging.

Eventually she acquired for me 'the perfect piece' and it cost £450.

Norman was appalled. He was perfectly content with his £100 piece on the north shore, alongside the place where the ferry one day is going to come in. And so far as I know he hasn't been to see it yet. Every time he sets out for Greece he stops short in Cannes, in the South of France. Very sensible of him. I (as you already know) am more of a pioneer; oh, a pioneer.

I was determined not to do anything illegal. Although I am a rebel I have a real horror of breaking the law. So Norman and I (using my shocking awful nose and sinuses and antrums as an excuse) applied to the Bank of England for permission to spend about £1,000 on building a little house on a Greek island. We said, if I recall, that the condition of my sinuses was deteriorating as a result of the English winters and I ought to winter abroad.

The Treasury pondered the whole matter long and deeply and then gave permission to the Bank of England. Who finally gave permission to me. Rena acquired a Greek lawyer to act as my proxy in registering the deeds for me on the nearby island of Skópelos. And then one day the deeds arrived, written all in Greek; I couldn't understand a blind word of them, except that my own name was mentioned.

A professional translation at £7 7s. per deed revealed that I owned 'an olive grove, washed on three sides by the Aegean Sea'. This seemed to me a bit expensive. So Dilys Powell, for love, translated the rest, between bouts of *My Word!*, and said that I seemed to have deeds to the land as far back as the sixteenth century. 'Just so long as I own it in the twentieth century,' I said to Dilys, in the bar of the Red Lion in St. James's Street, as we got ready to move across to the Piccadilly studio to do *My Word!*

'That's right,' said Dilys, abstractedly. 'Don't you think you ought to have a few words of Greek, dear?'

And there and then she wrote for me on a piece of paper:

Nay = Yes
Oichi = No
Ef Haristo = Thank you
Parakalo = Please
and Voeetheeay = Help

'There, dear,' said Dilys, kindly, as we passed back-stage amongst the kettles and drums and marimbas and vibraphones of the previous act who had used the studio, 'that should see you through pretty well anything in Greece.'

Chapter Nine

I Kept You an Olive Tree

Now my island was separated from me by a shimmering mist of light, reflected from the tumbling surface of the dark blue, dark green sea. It was smoother here, because we were sheltered by the land. Even at this distance from the island it was possible to see certain things.

I could see a rough red road, curving steeply above a series of beaches. I could see land that looked as though it had been farmed. Vineyards, hayfields, pine trees, water-melon fields lay there, smiling beneath the sun. Here and there, like a whitewashed box, there was an occasional house. Sometimes people moved, tiny as ants. It suddenly all seemed possible. Perhaps I too might own one of these white boxes one day.

Skiathos, the port, swam up, in a series of bright-coloured snapshots. Someone woke Granny and she came on deck and started waving her movie camera about. Boats, brilliantly painted and hung with bright sails; houses pink and green and blue washed; a chemist's shop with a big green cross; a green and yellow B.P. sign by a petrol pump . . . and then, on the quayside, rows and rows, ranks and ranks, of brown, closed, patient faces. Islanders who had assembled to see what manner of stranger the caique was bringing to their island.

They were fiercely dignified. Frighteningly shabby. The lads of the village wore cast-offs, handed down through generations from lad to lad. There were no lasses. Until I noticed this I had never really believed in the jealously guarded chastity of young Greek maidens.

We went ashore. I was so excited I hadn't noticed how cold it was. The sun shone, but didn't warm Granny. Her teeth were chattering. We walked along the quay towards a café. Rena and the proprietor greeted each other with rapture. We sat round a table. Cups of Turkish coffee appeared. Cheese, goats' cheese. More flinty bread. Granny (Turkish coffee hardly being the thing for diabetes) asked weakly could she lie down somewhere . . .

'Of course, of course,' said Rena. 'Your room is booked.'

And she leapt to her feet to lead the way to the rooms where (presumably) we were to spend the night. A shower of rubble fell all around us. A pick-axe broke through the wall a foot from my nose. Rena started to laugh, helplessly. Through her laughter she explained that the hotel where she had booked in was being pulled down. She had a foam-rubber mattress. Two small boys staggered under its weight. They led us to another house. And here, in a fairly icy room, overlooking the harbour, we popped Granny into bed. Braziers were brought in, full of glowing charcoal. 'You're not to go and see the land close to without me,' said Granny, but she was asleep before her cheek even hit the pillow.

Rena and I went out into the town.

We wound our way down side streets where half-skinned baby goats hung from nails in butchers' shops, where sacks and bins of corn lay open to the sky. It was all very wild and bizarre and terribly romantic, but it greatly resembled the Kasbah in Tangier. I suddenly longed irresistibly for Salford on a wet Saturday night.

Women with their heads wound in black scarves looked out at us over iron gates in gardens where oranges and lemons hung from trees. Fat men, in faintly discoloured shirts and woollen hats, slopped along in Turkish slippers behind mules. Bells rang incessantly.

'Could I pick a lemon?' I asked.

'Of course,' said Rena, and she called out something in Greek.

A pleasant man detached himself from a crowd of gawping onlookers, climbed a ladder, and gave me two of the biggest lemons I'd ever seen.

'No, no,' I said, feeling incredibly foolish. 'I meant I would like the feeling of the lemon *in my hand*, coming down from the tree. I want to pick it myself. I have never picked a lemon.'

They all shrugged their shoulders. They all raised their eyebrows. They all said 'Taxi-NAY', which is (I gather) Greek for O.K. So I raised my right hand, and shyly pulled. The lemon came away warm and firm and I had an absurdly over-emotional reaction. It fitted exactly into the palm of my hand. Two months later I used it, for lemon juice in a chicken fricassee when Jonnie and Sheila Van Damm and I ate Sunday supper. In retrospect it was the greatest lemon I have ever seen.

But at the time I was slightly perturbed by Skiathos. Everywhere we went people rushed at us and offered us houses for sale. Two shabby-looking villains ushered us into a very dark room, through a creaking door.

So far as I could judge, through the darkness, the room was entirely filled with chests of drawers and dressing-tables and chairs, pushed back against the wall to leave a space in the middle. I noticed a large fireplace, obviously unused. Inhabitants of Skiathos, both male and female, came pouring in, wearing black indistinguishable garments. They rubbed their hands, and twisted the palms, rustling like leaves beside us, peering anxiously through the gloom at the new, mad, English lady who had bought that bit of land, you know where, over by the lighthouse . . .

Appalled, I climbed a very rough ladder and stood by Rena on a half-finished floor of beams, showing huge chinks between the floorboards. We peered out, on to a lot of other roofs. One could only imagine that the sea lay somewhere behind them all.

'And how much do they want for this?' I asked.

'Five hundred pounds,' said Rena.

A good deal of giggling and cackling went on.

'Do you want it?' asked Rena.

'Good heavens no,' said I.

The whole tour of the village was like this. People constantly approached us, offering to sell something. Houses. Whole lambs. Potatoes. Milk. I bought some milk from a man with a crock on his back, drinking it gratefully from the big dipper at the side of the crock, staving off my hunger for a while. But, of course, the only thing I really wanted to do was to see that piece of land on the top of the cliff, which (according to those crazy Greek deeds) was *mine*.

We kept our promise to Granny. We woke her, and when she had failed to drink a cup of tea, and turned shuddering from another piece of goats' cheese, we set forth in Rena's car, zigging and zagging triumphantly along the only road in the island.

Eventually Rena stopped and we set off on foot. There was a track leading steeply down on the left. It went towards the sea through olive groves and ramshackle farm buildings. It wound in and out between goats tethered by the hind leg, chickens scratching, mules cropping, Greeks standing staring.

Soon the track left the inhabited part and began to climb steeply up the side of the cliff. Bulldozer tread-marks lay everywhere across the surface, which was pretty squelchy.

'I'm not a mountain goat,' said Granny, who was a bit silent after her sleep.

It was very cold. We climbed down a pleasant meadow, starred all over with buttercups and anemones.

We walked along a curving half-moon of beach. In the distance was my cliff, the cliff Rena had pointed out from the caique.

On top of the forty-foot-tall cliff, rough, gloriously overgrown with olive, oak, gorse and scrubby bushes of all sorts, was my land. It had been carefully divided off from everybody else's land with barbed wire. Wherever the surveyor had come on an olive tree he had wiggled the barbed wire round it, to avoid giving me an olive tree. So the perimeter of my land presented a very wobbly line indeed.

'Olive trees represent wealth to the peasants,' explained Rena. 'So they won't let you have one if they can help it. The oil pressed from the olives, the sale of it, is just about all they have to live on.'

'Until the tourists come,' I said.

'That's right,' said Rena.

'I'm not a mountain goat,' said Granny again, looking up to the cliff-top in some dismay. And she decided to go for a brisk, warming run along the beach. Rena, Kenneth Harper and I climbed through the gorse and scrub to the top of the cliff. We stood side by side, trying to visualise how a house would be when it was built there.

'The bulldozers will flatten it here and here,' said Rena.

'Look, there's a way down here to your own little private beach,' said Ken, sliding down a steep gully.

'Here, you can see, you will have the view of the village for your living-room,' said Rena.

Far on the horizon I could see the lace-white village of Skiathos. Could this ever be a living-room view? In between pale blue, pale green, pale silver was the sea. To left and right were the two tiny beaches where I hoped one day to swim naked at midnight if I wished, at noon if it wasn't too hot. Bang in the middle of the scrub, somehow missed by the surveyor's barbed wire, was a tiny olive tree.

'I told them to leave that tree,' said Rena. 'I *knew* you would like to have it growing up through your hallway.'

I sat down heavily in a gorse bush. But the hell of it was that Rena was absolutely right. It is now right through the middle of my hallway.

BOOK TWO

F. Harry Stone Is Greek
for Thank You

PROLOGUE

NEVER POINT A LOADED GREEK, EVEN IF HE ISN'T LOADED

I suppose I have had a few moments in my life that compare, emotionally, with this one. Standing there, waist-high in the green jungle-growth on top of that cliff, I actually visualised a house. I saw the view, framed in the imaginary open windows of a bedroom, a slightly different view from my study, a living-room with French windows opening on a veranda: and windows all along its right-hand side, looking down from the cliff-top to the sea.

Behind me, in my life, were other moments of such ecstasy. Moments when I recognised the struggle ahead and saw my goal in all its clarity. The moment when, writing my first book in a railway carriage between Manchester and Derby, I suddenly saw clearly that it was to be called *Thank You, Nelson* and why. The moment when I joined the *Daily Express* and the assistant editor, Harold Keeble, showed me the position in the paper I was to fill, and told me the paper's circulation was four and a half million.

The moment when I was in New York and the *News of the World* called for a thousand words on Marlene Dietrich to be cabled within the hour. And it is no use pretending I don't like the struggle that I recognise at such moments. The 'struggle' to me is everything. In all my forty-six years I have never enjoyed an achievement, nor even acknowledged it. Give me the struggle every time.

Scratched, bleeding, highly emotional, I now struggled down a gully to the right of the cliff to the water's edge, mainly on the seat of my jeans. Here, on a tiny, perfect half-moon of golden sandy beach, I might bathe and sunbathe one day. A white pebble shone amongst the sand. I picked it up and put it in my pocket.

We began to walk back to the village. All the way Rena talked land. Was I sure that this was the piece I wanted? Or should it go to James Jones, author of *From Here to Eternity*, who would otherwise have the bit we were walking through now?

I had met James in Paris and become very friendly with him and his wife Gloria, and I had seen him again in New York and asked him, 'Jim, do you want to buy a bit of a Greek island?'

Jim, with the wide, uncomprehending eyes of someone brought up on a farm, who has never correctly seen the sea, murmured, 'Yes . . . yes . . .' and had fallen into a deep stupor of delight. And in Jim I knew I had met an island maniac equal even to me.

'No, Rena,' I now said firmly. 'Let Jim have the bigger bit, because he will need a bigger house. I will stick to the bit I've got.'

All that evening I moved around in a daze. Rena and I bought lamb and jointed it up and we cooked a stew especially for Granny, with onions and peppers and carrots and celery and potatoes and *no oil*.

Granny was delighted.

Reeling slightly, and full of retsina and ouzo, I joined the men of Skiathos in a tavern. Here the silent engineer, with little pieces of paper and calculations on the backs of envelopes, involved me in a long discussion about my house and Jim Jones's house. Here I met a builder, eager to build both houses. He would start building right away. Sure. The house would be ready when I came back in May. Sure. Money, though – he needed money. I had £100 of travellers' cheques in my pocket for my journey around the world. Out they came and on to the table they went. Delight all round. More ouzo. Healths were drunk. (Ouzo is about as strong as Pernod, I suppose.) Somebody dashed off and fetched, I think, the mayor. Anyway, in came a huge, prosperous-looking fellow who seemed to act as banker to the entire island.

He heaved drachmai out of his pocket and took the travellers' cheques. I gave the drachmai to the builder. There was a lot of cheering. More ouzo.

'And this,' said Rena, with a great flourish, 'is Gus.'

I had already met Gus, back on the seashore at Pifki. He had come across in a second caique to meet Granny and myself. He is a tall, lean, charming man, in faded jeans and rimless glasses, and he speaks American very well indeed. He spent about twenty years of his life in the USA, learning about engines, motor-cars and farming. Now he has (he told me) a big cherry farm in Skiathos and his wife would very much like to sew the curtains for my new house. More ouzo.

Then the engineer's scowling face slowly cleared. He put down his envelope of calculations and joined in the general ouzo-induced hilarity. Hands were shaken all round. He began to talk rapid Greek, involving many sums of money. I have always been hopeless about arithmetic. For years I couldn't find my way around in New York because I don't *care* which numbers follow one another, and can't be bothered to count over twelve. And I remarked loudly, full of ouzo, something to this effect:

'If you build a good house for me for x drachmai, then my friend Jim Jones will want a bigger house for x plus y.'

The engineer suddenly looked delighted, smiled broadly, appearing quite attractive as he did so, and hands were shaken all around, and more ouzo was drunk.

Jim, my friend, wherever you are, when you read this, I apologise. You know (none better) how one can be led away in a foreign land, under public opinion, and how the mind explodes under the influence of raw native spirit, call it tequila or Pernod or absinthe or ouzo.

I am an idiot, and that's about it. In the dawn, the

following morning, itching all over, I left the island completely penniless.

We stole away into a rough sea, with a strong, swelling choppy movement, under the usual sickle moon.

I stayed on deck, peering through the darkness at my lovely, lovely land until the cold drove me downstairs into the little cabin, and there I found Rena and Granny tucked up, already feeling pretty sick. A dim light, in a whisky-bottle shrine to St. Andrew (fisher of souls) against the bulwarks, revealed their faces, yellowish through the gloom, and the driver, Sandeman's hat pulled down on his nose, in a crouching position between the two bunks.

The captain came aft with a tin jug of tea swilling about. On the surface, in the light of my electric torch, I could discern oil, faintly floating. *I* felt sick. Putting the tea down, I lurched out on the cold deck, holding a finger up Boy Scout fashion to see which way the wind was blowing, before I was sick into it. It was dead aft, bang astern.

'Quick, Rena,' I called down into the tiny cabin, sickness forgotten. 'Quick, what's Greek for sail?'

'Par-NAY,' replied Rena, without even opening her eyes.

So out on deck I went, shouting 'Par-NAY' to the skipper, and between us we pulled up, creakingly, the main par-NAY. And immediately the sea seemed calm. The boat stopped pitching and tossing. We sidled along quite fast, and the movement of the boat was reduced to that of a mere cantering horse. And neither Rena nor Granny nor I felt sick any more. I was surprised that the skipper hadn't thought of it for himself.

And I began to feel slightly less idiotic. After all, if I could think of an adroit bit of seamanship like *that* I couldn't be quite so dead stupid, even if I *was* itching all over . . .

And when we were back on the mainland again, and bowling along the main road back to Athens, mouths full of shashlik and beautiful soft white bread with poppy seeds baked on it, and herbs and lovely iced beer bought in Lafkardia, I began to feel downright clever.

There had been one beautiful moment. The driver had suddenly stopped abruptly, as if to turn round and go back, and indulged in a quick shouting match in Greek with Rena.

'What's going on?' Granny and I wanted to know, as Rena evidently shouted at him not to be silly, to hurry up, or else we would miss both ferry to Euboia and jet to Bangkok as well. 'What has he forgotten?'

'He says he has left his onions that he bought in Skiathos behind, on board the caique,' Rena explained.

'Onions,' said Granny, faintly. 'I'll give him bloody onions.'

Chapter One

Spain in Bangkok, Hong Kong, Tokyo

So there we were, Granny and I, airborne and leaving behind us the green isles of Greece. Granny sighed with joy as the sheer luxury of Air France enwrapped her, scented her with Chanel No. 5 and offered her champagne again. She buried her nose in a huge bouquet of parma violets that Mr Drakopoulos had handed her at the airport.

I was less happy. First of all, I was still itching. In the Grande Bretagne, in the bath, before we caught the jet, I had examined myself minutely in the mirror. I had nettle rash. I looked as if I had been beaten all over with whips. Weal upon red weal had risen, with white overtones, all over my back and stomach. Psychosomatic nettle rash. I have had it before, when I force my reluctant body to do something it doesn't really want to do. And two mornings' rising at 4 a.m. was not really restful. But most important of all I was leaving behind me the island of Skiathos, with which I was so deeply in love, and to which I was now so heavily and financially committed. What had I promised to send the builder? I dimly remembered shaking hands on a deal . . . but how much, and when, and particularly *how*?

As I wriggled and cursed and looked sideways out of the porthole Granny quietly took control.

'Go and have a big drink, dear,' she said. 'In that little bar at the back of the airplane. That should anaesthetise your nerves. They used to use whisky as an anaesthetic. Have plenty of Scotch. That will do you good.'

Good old Granny. Gratefully I lurched over her knees, miserably I groped my way back through the half-dark to the authentic Parisian-bar atmosphere. As the jet rose screaming through the night we stood hushed within, a little group of commercial travellers and drunks and tycoons in shirt-sleeves who always hang around in the bar of a long-distance jet. Soft French accordion music played. I might have been back in the bar of the Hotel Queen Elizabeth.

Gulping down the Scotch, I began to feel better. But my mental stability was rocky indeed. Below me somewhere, already probably far behind me, were the green, unforgotten Greek islands: one island, one dear and maddening island, in particular. Ahead lay Iran, Bangkok, Hong Kong, Tokyo, Alaska and the Pole before I could ever hope to see the bank manager and send funds to build my house.

'Know thyself,' says Apollo. 'Nothing to excess.'

And standing there sadly among my fellow sufferers I drank deeply (but not too deeply), wondering how long it would be before I managed to return to that cliff, those beaches, that idiotic wild olive tree. May, I promised myself. I shall return in May.

And oddly enough I kept my promise.

On we flew, over India. Unable to sleep, I peered down at the jungle. First grey-green jungle, dry and dusty, with immense empty brown river beds, hints of angry nine-armed goddesses of destruction and drought. Then dark green luscious jungle and the heat of Bangkok – a terrible humid body-blow below the belt.

Granny and I had an awful time in Bangkok. It was somewhere in the hundreds and no air-conditioning in sight. The hotel we had been booked into had never heard of us. Our mail and our cables went astray. The only time we could sightsee (and both of us were keen to sightsee) was at seven in the morning when we went to the floating markets and visited the Imperial Palace.

I was sitting panting in the moderately shady imperial garage, on the running board of the imperial Mercedes, waiting for Mr Averell Harriman (Ambassador at that time for the USA to the Far East) to get the hell out of the temple of the Emerald Buddha and let us poor suffering tourists in, when a lady approached me. Very friendly she was.

'I am from Seattle,' she said. 'My husband is an orthopaedic surgeon. We are travelling through the Far East examining "conditions". We were very shocked by Indo-China.'

Earlier in the year I had, with Ginette, addressed the Fashion Group of Seattle in a huge cinema at ten in the morning. The temperature had been about ten degrees below. I thought gratefully of Seattle and its cold, icy wind.

'Fancy,' I said, sitting there in my crumpled blouse and my dusty shoes and my creased white tropical skirt. 'I had the great honour and pleasure of addressing your fashion group this year.'

'Indeed,' she said, disbelievingly. 'And what fashion house do you represent?'

It was far too hot to explain. We passed on, sweating, into the temple of the Emerald Buddha, where we removed our shoes.

'Is this out of respect for the Buddha or to save floor-cleaning?' asked Granny. 'Anyway, the Buddha isn't even emerald. He's a sort of soapstone. Very disappointing.'

And that night, too, we went to a Thailand Cultural Evening. Dances, songs were announced. With many well-dressed American ladies and gents we poured into an air-conditioned culture hall. All the men wore dinner-jackets. All the women wore low-backed evening dresses. There was a general effect of tiaras.

A pretty young Thai lady stood and drew our attention to strange musical instruments like the 'Chortle Flute' and 'The Oom Boom Poom'. Granny and I were sitting next to an Australian called Charlie, who groaned. Every now and then he said 'Oh *Lord* . . .' under his breath. The evening dragged out, in all its cultural torment. And, covertly watching all the well-dressed ladies and gentlemen, I saw them wriggling. Then I saw them begin to scratch. And then something bit my ankle, and I slapped down *hard*. I killed the biggest Siamese flea you've ever seen.

On from Bangkok to Hong Kong we went, on this leg in a cosy B.O.A.C. jet where a steward said to me, in a sweet cockney voice, 'I wouldn't 'ave the beef if I was you, I think it's a bit off,' and filled me with deadly homesickness.

In Hong Kong I was received like royalty. The whole British colony there listen to *My Word!* once a week, so I found myself on television talking about Frank Muir and Denis Norden and Dilys Powell and their lovely person-alities, and in the huge double-bedroomed suite which I shared with Granny, back at the hotel, I constantly taped interviews for the radio. It was mildly frustrating. Outside, the streets of Hong Kong lay festering and in-spiring, filled with dubious glamour. The Kowloon ferry went to and fro. Junks shot across the harbour. And I was tied to a tape-recorder, to a TV studio. It did seem hard.

A charming one-armed Chinese gentleman called Mr Templo, who even surpassed Mr Drakopoulos for sweetness, came to take us out to dinner. Granny's parma violets were still with us, neck-deep in the bidet. Mr Templo was a walking example of Apollo's dictum: 'Know thyself – nothing to excess.' With his one arm he squired us around Hong Kong effectively and gently, doing more than most men could with two. And with such grace that after the first five minutes we had completely accepted the fact that to have one arm was rather grand.

At Aberdeen we ordered a sampan. We sat in three bamboo chairs. Behind us, bundled up in shawls, there was a baby. The sturdy young woman tugging away at the oar told Mr Templo it was hers. As she talked she propelled us with deft, almost contemptuous strokes across the water, beautiful with reflected lights, to the brilliantly lit barge where we were to dine. The girl, pulling at her oar, patted her stomach. She was proud that she was pregnant again.

We leapt ashore at the barge, helped by a fifteen-year-old. Mr Templo said this was our oarswoman's sister-in-law.

Then we had to pretend to choose our dinner from the huge floating larders alongside the barge. Squinting down into the green glowing depths, I could see huge crabs, monster lobsters, vast octopuses that had obviously been there, captive, patted and over-fed, for years. A boy with a fish-net lugged them up, dripping and dreadful, squirming with tiny parasites. Mr Templo explained that they were to be our dinner. I sincerely hoped not. There is nothing tougher than a lobster who has outgrown his strength.

Granny says that dinner consisted of those tiny squares of felt that used to be sewn on to the outsides of mattresses; ginger-flavoured. I can only remember the wild wine, in a tiny stone flask, that tasted of iodine and packed a kick like a mule.

Even without the wine Hong Kong delighted me. I loved the faint, brittle, salty, rotten smell of the sea. I loved the streets, all hung with banners, the floating population in the sampans who refused to have their photographs taken, lest our cameras should steal away their souls (exactly like Sir Laurence Olivier good-naturedly eluding the capture of autograph-hunters). I loved the flats, teeming with smiling faces, where I carelessly walked in someone's lunch, a few handfuls of filthy rice, drying on the pavement, and nobody minded. I loved the feel of the place, the restlessness, the ambition in the air. Yet almost directly, alas, we were airborne again, screaming away from Hong Kong towards Tokyo, once more with Air France.

The hostesses in our lovely jet had long ago changed from the neat navy-blue Air France uniforms into the full Japanese kit, hair-dos, obis and all, elegant over their behinds. Every now and then they passed among us with steaming hot towels, scented with eau de Cologne, so that we might rub the backs of our perspiring necks. Announcements were now made in Japanese over the tannoy. 'Dammy, Hammy, Shammy, Shonei!' they cried. And if anyone spoke to them they giggled. The giggle, I shortly learned from Pierre Guillery (who was the Mr Drakopoulos and the Mr Templo of Tokyo), is not a sign of Japanese joy or humour. It is a polite sign of embarrassment.

As Pierre met me at the Customs, talking impeccable Japanese, French and English, he started trying to explain to me about 'the soul of Japan'. For the next forty-eight hours he was steadily engaged in the same desperate ploy. Like all Frenchmen, he was a philosopher.

Tall, fair-haired, intellectual, extremely good-looking, he guided Granny and me into Tokyo. Through darkened streets, lively with coloured signs, over terrible road surfaces, with our springs screeching and protesting, we drove to our hotel. All the way Pierre tried to explain the Japanese.

'One day,' he said, 'that bomb fell on Hiroshima and the Emperor said: "I capitulate. Henceforth we will be a democracy." And these people, whose only life until that moment had been absolute obedience to the Emperor, were suddenly free. They had to make decisions for themselves. They had freedom of will. They didn't know what to do with it. They simply cannot think for themselves. They have to have a precedent.'

I tried hard to look intelligent. So did Granny.

'I have never heard of a rebel in Japan,' said Pierre. 'There would have to be a precedent for a revolution. And, anyway, how could you revolt and say you wanted the Emperor's law back again? The Emperor still *is* law. He had said everyone was to be a democrat. You can't really revolt back *into* the feudal system. How can you?'

Confused, Granny and I registered at our hotel.

A hotel, I may say, that was an almost perfect replica of a good American hotel, like the Hilton or the Sheraton-Cadillac at Detroit. Escalators ran from floor to floor. Doors opened by magic eye. The television could be controlled from the bed. Everything was padded with foam rubber. And in the morning the telephone began to ring. Every foreign journalist in Tokyo wanted to interview me about Prince Philip's remarks made that day about the *Daily Express*. That it was a 'bloody awful newspaper'. The fact that I no longer worked for the *Daily Express* made no difference. I rang Granny and explained what had happened.

'I will be on the television or taping interviews all day,' I explained.

'Thank God,' said Granny. 'So I can go shopping.'

That afternoon, when my news value and Granny's shopping urge had been exhausted, I went to see the Master of Aikidu, Mr Veshiba by name. Granny came back thrilled, with a lot of scarves, having made, as usual, instant communication.

Aikidu is a highly complex form of jiu-jitsu that embraces a complete philosophy of life, and Mr Veshiba is the master of it. We went to his establishment by underground tram, a fascinating experience, surrounded by nervous, spotty Japanese people, all apparently in the grip of some terrible neurosis. Outside in the streets the trees were covered in pink. I looked closer and found it was pink paper.

'Yes,' said Pierre Guillery. 'Typical Japanese. The cherry blossom was late this year, so they hang up paper blossom.'

Out in the suburbs we eventually found the equally paper-thin house of Mr Veshiba. We mounted a shallow step to a veranda and took our shoes off. Someone led us to an ante-chamber.

It was fascinating. There were hangings on the wall, examples of Japanese calligraphy, there were toys in the fireplace, as though children had left gifts. There were a few square hard pillows, one of which was red, to denote the guest of honour.

Suddenly a tiny little old gent came in. He was *really* tiny (about 4 ft. 10 in.), with a little straggling beard, long blue shapeless garments, under which I could vaguely discern a pair of wrinkled combinations. This was Mr Veshiba, Grand Master of Aikidu. Promptly, he fell flat on his face. So did we (Granny protested a bit). Pierre whispered to me, 'He is eighty-four years old.'

After a bit we all got up and sat on the cushions, cracking in the joints as we tucked our legs up under us. Veshiba made a long, long speech, which sounded very like the announcements on the jet, with variations: 'Dammy, Shammy, Hacki, Shucky, Highdi, Shaku.'

Pierre said: 'He says God is love. He is your father. You are his brothers and sisters. We are all married. There is no enemy. You must therefore never recognise the enemy. Never look him in the eyes. If he comes at you with all his strength you must absorb that strength until he becomes a part of you. So you will defeat him.'

Granny's elbows and knees cracked alarmingly. So did mine. I was glad when we got up and followed Veshiba into a gymnasium for a practical demonstration of the art, or the philosophy, or the game, or whatever the hell

I should call it. About forty or fifty young men, in long skirts and little padded coats, were hurling each other around. There were even two young women cautiously flinging each other to the ground. When the Grand Master entered everybody fell flat on their faces. So did we. Granny, under her breath, said it was a very silly custom.

Then a young man was told to attack the Grand Master. Blushing furiously, he did so. The Grand Master screeched, on a high-pitched note, and the young man collapsed in a heap. This went on for ages until Pierre asked, beamingly, 'Any questions?' Eventually, after some humming and hawing, I was allowed to go a round or two with the Grand Master.

The right clothes were brought. I was lashed into them.

'Now,' said the old boy, 'you attack me.'

I bowed low, and somewhat sanctimoniously.

'I couldn't possibly,' I said. (I was thinking of Pearl Harbour.) 'My philosophy of life would not permit.'

The old boy looked nonplussed for a second, and then laughed happily. He told Pierre I was a Grand Master already and should instruct *him*. And for half an hour or so we skipped around each other, occasionally rolling on our backs with our paws in the air, like Yorkshire terriers waiting to have their tummies rubbed. At the end of the session my admiration for Veshiba knew no bounds. If at the age of eighty-four *I* am able to skip about like this I shall be more than contented.

That evening Pierre took us on a tour of the Tokyo coffee houses. We visited the Communist headquarters and heard the boys and girls intoning the tune I know as 'Midnight in Moscow'. We visited a very odd ice cream parlour where yellow and red winking lights squirted on and off in time to the tune of Noel Coward's 'Mad About the Boy'. And finally in Le Club Jazz some tiny Japanese musicians in blue dinner-jackets played a neat, over-rehearsed and utterly lifeless version of (of all things) 'South Rampart Street Parade'.

That was the moment at which I at last grasped the message that Pierre Guillery had been trying to teach me about the soullessness of Japan.

'I am sorry I have been so slow,' I said to Pierre. 'There is nothing spontaneous anywhere in Japan? That is what you have been trying to tell me, isn't it? That they can never become artists, nor have an original thought, because they can never get out of control, because "out of control" would terrify them to death? They only want to copy, copy, copy and stay in line and rehearse. They can never, as you or I can, escape *into* anything?'

Pierre was delighted.

He patted me excitedly on the shoulder.

'Good . . . good!' he cried. 'Did discipline always annoy you, then? Tell me what you mean by out of control and by escaping *into* something? Discipline is rather charming in its own right, though, isn't it, don't you think?'

And slowly, haltingly, because it was so much in my

mind, I began to tell Pierre what I meant by 'out of control' and 'escaping into something'.

'Well,' I began, 'you see, I bought this Greek island . . .'

THE SUN ALSO KEEPS ON RISING AND RISING AND RISING AND RISING . . .

I longed to stay in Tokyo and go on exploring the Japanese soul. But because of the tyranny of my deadlines we had to leave it behind us. Granny had begun to sigh as we took off on our penultimate leg to Alaska over the Pole. We had two breakfasts that morning, one in Alaska and one in Hamburg.

It was also her penultimate leg, poor Granny. She had begun to reach the limits of her physique. Both of us needed hair-dos. As I hurried her across tarmac after tarmac, into exotic city after exotic city, I would grip her under the elbow.

'Come on, Gran,' I would say. 'Go it, love. Keep it up, Gran. Come on, love . . .'

And, unflinching, Granny would stumble wearily up the steps into the jet, brighten visibly at the luxury of Air France, and then fall into a heavy doze between the endless helpings of rich, rich food. *My* stomach had long ago refused to take it. I was living on cheese and apples, washed down by champagne. And, because I simply cannot help looking out of the windows of an aircraft, I couldn't, *wouldn't* sleep. Wide-eyed, bleary-eyed, I stared down at the earth as it spun away beneath us. I stared at the twilight of the Polar regions: grey, grey, grey, with nothing to break the monotony of the ice, except an occasional crevasse, 'cwavasse' as Marlene calls them.

Dimly I could hear the brown velvet tones of her voice telling how she had saved the lives of a crew of the Dakota flying low over the ice in World War II.

'The guy said to me, "Pwepare to abandon aircwaft." And I had been reading this book which said: "In no event abandon aircwaft over ice, else you will fall into a tewwible *Cwavasse* and never come out any more . . .

'So I said to him, "Look here, I am much older than any of you guys, let me come up fwont and see if there's anything I can do." So I went up fwont, into the cabin. And sure enough it was all iced up, and no one could see out. So I took my little hair-dwyer and I defwosted the cabin . . ." '

And as the jet flew on, and I looked down on the ice, which had formed itself into fantastic shapes, drifts and banks like ghosts under the polar winds, I began to prepare myself for a long, long struggle over my house.

First that land, all maquis-grown, would have to be cleared and bulldozed flat.

'That's all right,' Rena had said cheerfully. 'The Army will do that for us. The captain in charge of the bulldozers is my very good friend, and he will do it for you as he did it for me, while he is building the General's Road.'

The General's Road was to stretch right around the cliffs where Jim Jones and I had chosen our land, right round the cape that stuck out into the sea above the lighthouse, until it connected up with the General's House. This had been presented to the General by a grateful Greek Government. And we would be lucky enough to have the benefits of the road. Until it was built all the building materials would have to come on muleback to my little peninsula, on muleback or by boat.

And the whole thing was going to take place fifteen hundred miles away. It seemed impossible that it should ever be done, without supervision, without adequate praise, day after day, without 'drinks all round' and 'a feast for the builders' when they put the rafters in . . .

I remembered the Army, and the captain in charge of the bulldozers. He was a handsome well-dressed man, with becoming scarlet tabs, whom I had last seen standing negligently graceful by his tents.

I longed to be there when the bulldozers ripped into the surface of my jungle. I wondered would they spare my olive tree. I wondered if wild olive trees produced fruit, or would they have to be grafted. I thought in terms of terraces, tiny vineyards, leading down to the sea, where one day I could have a little landing stage for motor boats, a diving place, into nine feet of exquisite turquoise water. And as I thought, and drew little plans on my knee, and imagined the cool breeze floating through my living-room, someone came back into the jet and interrupted my dream to bring me forward to the cockpit.

Because we were flying over the Pole the sun had just risen for the second time that Wednesday morning. It hung, like a huge golden pear, just above the horizon to our left. The moon, a tiny silver nutmeg, was nearby.

The No. 1 Pilot waved at them.

'I always think of that great line of Victor Hugo's,' he said. ' *"La lune, négligement jetée sur le ciel"* . . .'

'Ra-ther,' I said, enthusiastically. 'Ra*ther.*'

But I thought I would be much happier if the No. 1 Pilot would just keep his mind on his instruments and his navigator's calculations, and not bother with reciting the great lines of Victor Hugo. He sat there, staring out at the unbelievable beauty of the navy-blue clouds, the greying sky, and murmured poetry. And I thought it was almost as bad as when the captain of an aircraft walks through the aircraft greeting the passengers and passing the time of day (or night) with them.

On these occasions I always long to screech out, 'Go back . . . go back, for God's sake, to your joystick and your steering gear and control this plane in person!'

We breakfasted for the second time in Hamburg, flirted with the storms in the North Sea and set down in Paris in time for me to telephone copy to the *News of the World.* Then, more dead than alive, Granny and I sat with Ginette in an Italian restaurant eating spaghetti. Ginette found us odd companions. Granny kept nodding off to sleep and I was utterly obsessed by the problems of building drains in a house where there was no main sewer and where I was determined not to pollute my own sea-bathing.

Fortunately for me, a new friendship was just around the corner on my return. I got to know Sir Basil Spence, the greatest architect in England, who had just designed Coventry Cathedral.

Chapter Two

Sir Basil to the Rescue

Chronologically Sir Basil Spence only enters this saga when the foundations had been laid, when the walls (very nasty they looked, too, in their pink honeycomb brick, brittle and pathetic and half finished) were up.

Granny went straight into hospital 'for observation' to have her diabetes sorted out. I used to go and see her, sitting up in bed, bright-eyed and much rested. I evidently hadn't killed her, thank goodness.

Various friends visited Skiathos before I went back again. All were enthusiastic amateur cameramen. They took photographs and films of varying horror, they then rang me up and tormented me, talking long and with enthusiasm about *their* architect, *their* land and *their* plans. No one could ever satisfy me about my drains. Everyone seemed to be buying land. My old colleague from the *Daily Express* days, Harold Keeble, bought land and suggested his wife Susan should travel to Greece with me. Susan Keeble invited me to a party to meet others who were all talking about buying land. Jim and Gloria Jones clinched *their* deal. Peter Guttman of Hammond and Hammond (Publishers) clinched his. Peter Bull bought some and wouldn't tell us where, but it was much cheaper than anything we had managed. We all bought 'Teach Yourself Greek Conversation' gramophone records and went around murmuring 'Kali MAY-ra . . . Kali SPAY-ra . . . Kali NICKtay' to each other.* I discovered all the waiters at the Ivy were Greek, and practised on them. The whole world seemed to be on a Greek-island-buying jag.

Rena Harper came and went, pink-cheeked and triumphant, still enthusiastic, laughing heartily, always in a good temper, always pouring ouzo and heavily laden with furniture, food and stores for her own house. Every now and then however even Rena expressed bewilderment at her beloved island.

'Try not to get stranded on Skiathos in Holy Week,' she told me on one of these flying visits. 'All they eat that week is beans. And black beans at that.'

My first opportunity to see for myself what in hell had happened to the drains didn't come until May, when my plans were laid to drive in a hired Volkswagen Slumberwagon across France to Marseilles where I would take a Greek freighter to the Piraeus. Rena was to accompany me on this trip. So was Sue Keeble. They were enthusiastic about it. Then they decided to fly. More comfortable. I can hardly blame them. I was left without

---

* *Good morning. Good afternoon. Good night.*

travelling companions. Jonnie was convinced I should not go alone.

'You are not to do it,' she told me. 'You must find someone – and quickly . . .'

It was while I was casting round in my mind who could possibly put up with a Mediterranean trip on a Greek freighter that I got to know Basil Spence.

I was writing a series for *Woman* magazine and Sir Basil was one of the people with whom (I had said) I would like to spend an evening. Greatly daring, I wrote to him, called on him in his house in Canonbury Square, took him and his wife Joan out to dinner, dined with them several times, spent a weekend at their house on Beaulieu Water. We even went to Chichester together to see Olivier and Plowright and Redgrave in *Uncle Vanya*. What with one thing and another we were more or less inseparable all through that spring.

Basil, early on in the relationship, expressed fascination at the thought of someone building a house fifteen hundred miles away without an architect. (The scowling engineer in the back of the Cadillac had gone, none knew whither. As he was unable to speak or write English, I was never able to find out where or why.)

'You see, dear,' Basil said to his wife, as we sat gorged and helpless after one of our enormous meals, 'it is as I have always said. There is no necessity for architects.'

Behind Basil's head there was the cartoon of the great tapestry by Graham Sutherland which now hangs in Coventry Cathedral. All round him, in his beautiful drawing-room, there was evidence of buildings and homes created and planned, right down to the very last item of taste and texture, right down to the wood used for the dining-room table. There could have been no greater contrast to my haphazard goings-on in Greece.

Basil is a huge man, lion-like, with a fine yellow beard, like an Elizabethan sea captain with his big, comfortable pleasure-loving tummy and his blazing blue eyes. When Basil starts twinkling there is no greater charmer in the world.

'Oh dear,' I said. 'I do wish you were right. It seems to me I need an architect very much, even if it's only for drains. I suppose you have drains in Coventry Cathedral?'

'Indeed we do,' said Basil. 'And do you know who is the only person who has ever enquired about them before? Princess Margaret.'

So I told Basil all about my drains. Or, rather, my lack of them.

'I'm sure there aren't any,' I said. 'I'm sure they are going to put in a bathroom and a lavatory and a kitchen sink and then just have the water running about outside, all greasy and worse, all over the garden . . .'

'But haven't you taken *advice*?' asked Basil, appalled.

'Well,' I said. 'Every time I ask anyone about them somebody says, "In Greece we always put our drains in last."'

Basil laughed long and loud. But he took it all very seriously indeed. The next time I saw him, in his 'folly' house on Beaulieu Water, he was sitting in an old green woolly fisherman's jersey peeling shrimps for lunch.

'And how are your Greek drains?' he asked, without preamble.

I shrugged my shoulders.

'A friend came back from Skiathos this month,' I said, 'and he showed me a picture of the foundations of the house. It looks as though it is going to be marvellous. It shows an olive tree, growing up where the entrance is going to be. And he took a movie too. And the movie shows a man digging in the bottom left-hand corner. But there's nothing to show *what* he is digging.'

Basil neatly decapitated a shrimp, pulled off his tail and ate him, smiling broadly.

'He might be digging your grave?' he suggested, mildly. Joan came out of the kitchen.

'Basil,' she said, 'you must do something to help Nancy. You must do something at once.'

'I have,' said Basil, decapitating another shrimp. 'I have written to Doxiadis.'

Now Doxiadis is an architect of such splendour that the name Sir Christopher Wren pales to insignificance beside him. Basil had, it now seems, written to him explaining what had happened and asking for a report. An assistant would be asked to go to Skiathos and inspect everything. Doxiadis! This was taking a trip-hammer to kill a butterfly with a vengeance.

'Well,' said Basil, 'all we can do now is to wait for the report, that's all. There's nothing we can do. Of course, you will see the house for yourself in May, but I do think you should have an expert opinion.'

Inarticulate with gratitude I helped Basil decapitate the last of the shrimps. Then we ate them. Then we crossed Beaulieu River to Lord Montagu's house and there wildly water-skied. I can't say I care for it very much. Too wet, too cold and too exhausting round the knees. But oddly enough I found it quite easy to balance and quite easy to stand on the water. And with all the activity I forgot all about Doxiadis. I even became confused over his name (which was terrible of me) and made matters worse by referring to him as Archimedes.

And my Greek departure date, 20th May, came inevitably nearer. My life at this point was complicated by the opening of the musical show called *Little Mary Sunshine* into which I had put some money. Granny followed suit. So did Jonnie. So my departure for the Isles of Greece was overshadowed by a flurry of first-night parties and the wildness of 'having become an angel'.

One of my American friends, Alfred Allan Lewis, turned up in time for the first night. And he, startlingly enough, 'volunteered' for the trip in the Greek freighter. (In actual fact, as I recall, the poor boy was 'pressed' into the service. I took him to lunch and said, 'We're going to Greece,' and he replied, 'Aw right.') So my two lists (Those who Want Seats for the First Night and What to Take in a Caravan for Greece) kept on muddling one another up and getting hopelessly intermingled.

Alfred Allan Lewis is a big boy who is inclined to

over-weight. He writes plays. When he is over-weight he looks like a son of Robert Morley's or a version of the young Oscar Wilde before the moths got at him. When he is slim he is quite handsome. On the Greek trip (he had two plays under option, one to Michael Redgrave and one to an American producer called Norman Twain) he was on the wagon and had given up smoking. So he got quite thin and all the clothes which he had worn at the age of eighteen at college fitted him. He swanked about this until one day he caught his exquisite beige tropical trousers in a bit of the Volkswagen that stuck out and rent them, clew to earring.

We went to inspect the Volkswagen together, taking Jonnie and Michael Griffiths, the art editor of *She*. We went to the Army and Navy stores to buy a spade, a canvas bucket for water, a tent, two sleeping bags, pillows, stores. Together we compiled list upon list of necessary food, drink, knives, forks, spoons. From time to time I explained about the first time I had met Alfred Allan.

We went to a performance of the film of *Romeo and Juliet*. The old film, with Norma Shearer and Leslie Howard and John Barrymore. And about halfway through we both got fed up with it, rose to our feet and left, leaving our mutual friend, Fred Sadoff, Michael Redgrave's partner, to sit the film out all by himself. So we knew we had pretty well the same reaction to everything. Moreover, Alfred Allan was a man of parts. There was little he had not done. He had even, for a mad season, been in Mae West's *Diamond Lil*. I love to put him on, and have him tell this story, which he does extremely well:

'I was walking along Broadway,' he says, 'when a man said to me, "Wantawork nights, bud?"; so I said, "What at?" "In a show," he replied. He took me to audition in the gents' lavatory in the Booth Theatre and there I met Mae West. She said, "He'll do," and poured me into the tightest suit you've ever seen. I was "Mister Muscles, da Champ". For weeks I strutted across stage in that suit, the tightest suit, so tight I could hardly move my legs. The lines that accompanied my strut were "Dere goes da champ, Mae", to which she would reply "Huh", and then someone would say, "Wanta feel his muscles, Mae?" and she would reply, 'It's not his muscles I wanta feel" . . . which would bring the house down. Well, now. At my début the whole of my family, my entire family from Brooklyn, all my aunts and uncles, and, of course, my *mother*, were on hand in the stalls to see the boy making good. The boy in his first role. And Mae West said *that* . . . Can you imagine the gasp of horror that went up from my assembled family?'

As I write, Alfred Allan has another play under option, this time to David Susskind, so he may well have out-grown that charming period in his life when he had all the time in the world on his hands and so was able to drop everything (except his rewrites for Norman Twain) and come to Greece with me.

'Together we made lists.
Then we made lists of lists.
Then we lost the lists.'

Alfred Allan's list started 'Revolver, Hunting Knife, Bisquits, Flash Light, Matches', so I pointed out that 'Biscuits' wasn't spelled that way, but stood for 'Twice cooked' and Allan shrugged his heavy shoulders. 'Aw right,' he said. *My* list started 'Foam Rubber Mattress, Tent, Wine', and Allan pointed out that I had spelled 'Mattress' wrong. We glared at each other. Perhaps we shouldn't go? Jonnie restored peace between us and struck 'revolver' off both our lists. 'Ridiculous,' she said. And then we dragged the Volkswagen out of its garage by Brews' European Cars and examined it.

It had a bench driving seat made of some sort of plastic. This got very sticky indeed in heat and should have been covered with something sensible like cotton that absorbs perspiration, only we never thought of it. It had a tiny kitchen, with two Calor-gas jets and a huge living area that could be occupied by a bed, also lit by Calor gas. There was a luggage rack on the roof (which turned out to be rather frail) but there was also adequate storage space in the living area for suitcases and packing cases full of food. And then I was approached by a supermarket chain who thought it would be a good publicity stunt if N. Spain 'kitted up' for her trip for Greece.

Alfred Allan and I drove out to Hounslow one day to the supermarket.

We began in a quiet way of business.

The manager approached us and said, 'Do please help yourselves.' We got three little wagons and began to push them gently round the stores. 'Come on,' said the manager. 'Don't be shy. Be my guest.' And we began, slowly at first, and then, as the madness of the thing began to hit us, faster and faster, and greedier and greedier, to snatch, snatch, snatch from the shelves. We took hunting knives, serving knives, packets of Chow Mein, bottles of Marron paste for chestnut goodies, soap flakes, detergents and a strange thing called 'Bubble Your Baby Clean'. We took dried stewing steak (only add water), rice, cake mix, powdered milk, tinned milk, beer, sugar, tea, coffee, mops for washing-up and some light-weight aluminium deckchairs. We took toothpaste, shaving cream (Alfred Allan), toothbrushes, washing soap, face flannels, sponge bags, tinned ham, tinned tongue, meat loaf, curry (dried, just add water), soup, soup, soup. We took . . . Well, we took plenty. The manager's hair stood on end when he saw our little wagons. What had been intended as a free and generous gift had somewhat outrun itself. We both cleared our throats.

'I think you'd better give me a bill,' I said.

His face cleared.

The bill came to fifty-seven pounds fifteen shillings and sixpence. And the irony of it all was that we needed so little of any of this. We never slept in the Volkswagen. We slept on the beach on the beautiful bouncy mattresses. The wine curdled on the road. And Alfred Allan took the hunting knife and (trying to test the level of the petrol with it) dropped it quietly into the petrol tank. For all I know it is there yet.

PUT THAT ANGEL DOWN, YOU DON'T KNOW WHERE SHE'S BEEN

I cannot, at this stage of the game, really explain how I became one of *Little Mary Sunshine's* angels. 'Little Mary Worry Guts', as Denis Norden used to remark cheerfully of the whole enterprise.

For I rather dislike the theatre. (I love theatrical people, that's quite different.) That lighted box, with all those excessively extroverted people hopping about up there beyond the footlights, and us expected *to pay* and stay still while, with a few exceptions, such as *A Man for All Seasons* and *Uncle Vanya*, they talk. The theatre has bored me more than anything else that passes under the name of entertainment. Movies I love. Circuses don't worry me. Horse shows are spiffing. I even like American football on TV. But oh how often I have groaned at the theatre!

So how in the hell did I actually put *money* into the theatre? Good money? Money I had *worked* to get?

Well, my father had a sweet light baritone singing voice, and in some of the numbers of *Little Mary Sunshine* I could hear echoes of my father's voice. It was an untried, untouched tinka-tink baritone that used to croon to his 'Lindy Lou', or his 'Little Dolly Daydream', or even ask his pretty maiden if there was anyone at home like *You*: and when the male chorus in *Little Mary Sunshine* sang:

> 'I'll walk you up the garden path
> And watch the birdies have a bath . . .'

I was always conjured back to sit with my father under a childhood sky in the garden of the rectory at Greystead in Northumberland on the North Tyne, where a robin would fly and hop, nearer and nearer, listening to my father's song.

> 'Tell me, pretty maiden, is there
> Anyoneathomelikeyou?'

And the robin would alight on Father's foot, and cock his head on one side, bright black eyes bulgeous with joy as my father sang all through his repertoire.

I would have loved my father to hear *Little Mary Sunshine*. He would have adored it all: the virtuous heroine (Miss Patricia Routledge in a blonde wig looking fearsomely like Miss Jeanette MacDonald), the charming young ladies of the chorus, the foolish songs 'Look for a Sky of Blue' and 'Colorado Love Song'.

Because of these haunting echoes I would sit entranced through *Little Mary*. I also fought for it, dragged people to see it (my unfortunate friend Laon Maybanke, the photographer, had to endure it three times and Alfred

Allan Lewis five) and forced it down the throat of any theatrical critic I happened to know. Goodness, what a bore I was! However, my enthusiasm was not, alas, shared by the general public.

For a start the general public could not make head nor tail of it. And they were very upset by the antics of the 'little public' of pros and semi-pros who camped their way steadily through every performance and bewildered the general public with their squeals and shrieks. The general public were often heard to say '*Shush*' quite loudly to a member of the 'little public'.

Then, to go on with, the show was written by an American about America: and where the English will protect their own they will not bother too much with Americans.

Finally, it was somewhat over-lavish in production, mounted a huge orchestra, expensive scenery and costumes. It might well have been just as effective (and a darned sight cheaper for Granny and Jonnie and Ginette and me) if it had been performed against one single backdrop with a talented old lady at the piano and a bright young man at the drums. Or not performed at all.

But when Alfred Allan and I set out in our Volkswagen the show seemed well and truly launched. It had a moderately good press. So we stuck the photographs of my favourite *Sunshine* episodes on the windscreen and watched them yellow and wither and crinkle in the suns of France, Italy and Greece.

We left on a Saturday afternoon and got hopelessly

lost in Regent's Park, looking for the road to Southend. Ginette had suddenly panicked and telephoned that every airport in France was going on strike, so we must hurry, hurry, hurry . . . But, even so, as we drove round and round Queen Mary's rose garden, I said to Alfred Allan, 'Look here, there's just time to go into the matinee and see they're all right.'

Instead of his usual easy-going 'Aw right', Alfred Allan was quite firm.

'Come on, now, Nancy,' he said. 'If we don't leave now we'll never catch that plane . . .'

So leave we did. Into the gathering dusk, above the reflections of the sunset in the broad and fascinating mouth of the Thames, over shipping and wrecks and piers and sand-bars we flew. Out of England. Into France. To Paris. To the South. To Skiathos.

Chapter Three

A Turn to the Wight

Alfred Allan wanted to know why we went to France via Southend and Calais. 'Seems to me,' he said, sweetly reasonable, 'that we are going north to get south. Is there an explanation for this?'

Well, yes there was. Ever since Freddie Laker, the dashing millionaire tycoon behind the Channel Air Bridge, and all the other British independent airlines, had allowed me to do the Arc de Triomphe to Marble Arch Air Race with him, I had always gone Southend–Calais. Southend Airport belongs to Freddie's company and we entered the race to fly from there to prove it was much faster as a route than Lydd-Le Touquet. 'Why,' I said, 'we even beat Stirling Moss.'

Alfred Allan was unconvinced. Shouting away to me, lashed into his seat-belt in the utterly unpressurised cabin of the Bristol freighter, he announced that he was pretty sure I had left something out of the story.

And so I had, of course, so I had. On that racing occasion we had flown from Southend to Le Bourget, after scattering traffic on the Southend road as if we were the

Surrey with the Fringe on Top. We had a motley band
of passengers, too. Colin Hodgkinson, legless pilot from
World War II who had tried to kick a gate down with
his tin legs. Champion cyclist Eileen Sheridan and her
son. *Her* legs had come up in terrible nerve rash. Freddie's wife Joan. And a correspondent from *The Times*
who had been quietly sick into a paper bag most of the
way while we shrieked, '*Par-donnez-moi, c'est la course!*'
out of the window.

'I see,' said Alfred Allan, as we disembarked at Calais,
as Mr Bell, the port officer, hurtled us through Customs.
'I see. That does make all the difference.'

I refused to drive in the twilight, so we turned off the
road to a huge, superb dinner in Montreuil and after that
we took the road. Goodness knows I have often driven
the NI to Paris. I really know this road by heart. But
that night there was a full gale blowing, which tried hard
to hurl the Volkswagen off course, just as if she were a
top-heavy Spanish galleon. The moon fled across the sky,
clouds around her, like an over-painted, over-romantic
backdrop to *Giselle*. The trees bent themselves double.
The rain occasionally lashed. The headlights picked up
hedges, village streets, deserted and scarcely lit. Names
from both world wars went flying by under the moonlight.

Eventually we made the outskirts of Paris. Somewhat
bewildered, I missed the turn on to the Boulevard and
the Gate of St. Ouen, and at one o'clock in the morning
we were hopelessly lost, somewhere around the Gare
du Nord. Heaven knows how we extricated ourselves,

for I cannot recall dropping Alfred Allan off at the Hotel Queen Elizabeth. But I do recall whimpering gently as I slid off to sleep in Ginette's spare room. (This is the same room known to Noël Coward as 'my sweet'. He once rang Ginette from Switzerland and asked, 'How is my suite?' and Ginette replied, 'Very well, thank you,' before she realised he meant the room.)

We lunched next day with Paul-Emile and Ginette. Marlene invited herself to lunch. This delayed our departure for almost a day, because Marlene was such good value. She had a long story to tell about some theatrical management which began: 'And I said to him: "*Si j' étais putain*, schweetheart . . ." ' Also she seemed to think I could help her get some relation of General de Gaulle's a job in England, and a series of frighteningly silly telephone calls took place between Paris and London, where Jonnie (at a press reception in the Savoy Hotel) was stunned to receive Marlene's dark, plum-cake-coloured tones. From time to time I would grip the telephone, saying such things as, '*Madame, pardon, je parle Français si malheureusement, je park comme une bête . . .*' sending Marlene off into gales of laughter. Once she said: 'Look, can't we just leave a message? Then we won't have to go through the *malheureusement* bit again?' I will do a great deal to make Marlene Dietrich laugh. When she laughs she looks like a child and her eyes disappear into her head, and she shakes all over with joy. To see Marlene break up like that I would spend more than a day on the telephone.

Anyway, by the time we managed to pull out on to the Avenue Marceau it was pouring with rain. Marlene had attired herself from head to foot in kinky black mackintosh. Like a very sprightly advertisement for Skipper sardines, she clambered into the back. Ginette clambered up too. Amidst the cooking pots and pans these two elegant women drove with us to the House of Pierre Balmain. At this point Marlene suddenly recognised the whole enterprise.

'But where are you going?' she asked.

'To Greece!' screeched Ginette.

'To Gweece! Good gwacious!' murmured Marlene.

Looking at her covertly in the driving mirror I could see that she was laughing again.

'Marlene,' I asked her. 'Why when you are singing "My Blue Heaven" do you put out your *left* hand when you sing "A Turn to the Right?" '

'Because it is the audience's wight,' said Marlene, surprised. I stopped the Volkswagen on the corner of the Avenue Pierre Premier de Serbie and the Avenue Georges Cinq. The entire hotel staff of the Queen Elizabeth were out on the pavement to wave us goodbye. Jaws dropped, eyeballs started, as Marlene's famous legs climbed gravely down from the Volkswagen to the kerb. Hugging, kissing, in which Monsieur Rambaud, the concierge, my friend, seemed to join.

'A Turn to the Wight!' we cried. I put out my left hand and turned to the left.

Ginette and Marlene stood on the pavement shouting.

I think they shouted 'Write! Write!' but Alfred Allan says it was 'Wight . . . wight.'

It rained all the way to the autoroute. It rained all the way down the autoroute to Fontainebleau. It rained all the way to Pouilly, where I paused and bought two bottles of Pouilly Fumé. They jerked, jiggled, jumped and frothed themselves up alarmingly until they were in an almost total state of undrinkability.

We stayed that night in a fearful hotel, escorted through the darkness to the annex by a fretful youth in shirt-sleeves. It was raining, of course. Has there ever been a time, on the journey south, when I haven't put up for the first night in some hotel annex full of crumbs, with rain lashing on the windows, and the huge *camions*, French lorries like primeval beasts, thundering by?

But in the morning, after seven hours of dreamless sleep, I was full of hope.

And all the way south we sang (terribly) 'A Turn to the Wight' and 'You-oo-oo and I-eyeye will li-hi-hive and die, Underneath a Colorado sky' until suddenly at lunchtime we were in Lyons and the sun *was* suddenly shining, and Alfred Allan clambered down and picked his way across tram tracks, and came back with a sheet of paper, wrapped round bread and cheese and huge, wet black cherries.

The Seidmanns had suggested we went to Les Baux: so after an abortive stop in Montelimar, where we sent postcards to the entire *Little Mary* company with '*Look!* for a Sky of Blue' scribbled on them, we wriggled our way down the valley of the Rhone and inspected Les Baux. We thought it a terrible place.

Not content with the phoney ruins they already had there, they seemed to be building some new ones. The sun was setting, so we found a good, clean, quiet, sensible hotel called Les Antiquités. It was actually an aristocratic converted château, with baths and dinner for about a pound a night.

'Leave it to me,' cried Alfred Allan, flourishing the communal privy purse, of which he was in command, 'and we will leave France quite rich!'

We had two days before our freighter sailed from Marseilles, and we spent them at Cassis – the fishing village which was once done over by Josh Logan and the *Fanny* company. Leslie Caron, Maurice Chevalier, Charles Boyer, Horst Bucholz and Lionel Jeffreys had cavorted there and I had joined them to write a story.

The Hôtel de la Plage was as good as ever. The windows opened on to the Mediterranean, as ever. And Madame (who runs the Hôtel de la Plage) was only vaguely disconcerted when the huge Alsatian that she keeps for just such a purpose leapt from behind the keyboard and fastened its fangs in my ankle. I bled profusely, as I always do. I thought Alfred Allan was a bit unsympathetic about this.

In my mind's eye, as Alfred Allan and I wandered to and fro along the beach road, I could in retrospect hear Josh Logan expounding his great thesis on the work of Marcel Pagnol, the man who wrote *Fanny*.

'This man wrote great tragic themes,' cried Josh. 'The story of Fanny and one man fathering another man's child *is* a great tragic theme. But Pagnol told his story in terms of low, wonderful bucolic comedy. That's what the Marseillais and the Provençals are like. Great big personalities and characters, all richly comic. waiting to be deflated with a hat-pin. Pagnol used a very loving hat-pin, too.'

Alfred Allan and I wandered to and fro, from port to hotel, passing and re-passing a Tennessee Williams type house, filled with layabouts and the whining noise of Algerian music. Sometimes, too, there was low moaning within. Always the windows peered out like black, empty eye-sockets, as we punctured one another's fantasies with a loving hat-pin.

It rained once or twice. I saw a man gathering snails after the rain. I remembered how Josh used to take me to the rushes of the film in the tiny half-disused little flea-pit cinema, descending abruptly from a farmyard where cocks crowed and hens scratched. I sat with Chevalier outside a bar, and the British fleet came in. Three sailors asked Maurice for his autograph, and he gave it, writing with a huge flourish of his smooth-writing golden pen: 'Maurice Chevalier, Admiral of the Fleet.'

Alfred Allan and I sat in the sun and lay on the shingle. We studied, through half-lowered eyelashes, the unfortunate British tourists staggering along the front, heavily laden under rucksacks, climbing boots and peeling sunburn. By the time the freighter was ready to sail from the

'Mole of the Piraeus' at Marseilles it was 25th May and Lord Beaverbrook's birthday.

In a perfect wallow of sentimentality I towed Alfred Allan around Marseilles until I found a post office, and so could send Beaverbrook a cable of congratulations.

It is hard to explain my personal devotion to Beaverbrook. I haven't worked for him now for several years. I left him one Christmas for a variety of reasons, not the least of which was that my own usefulness to him was used up. But my fondness and admiration for him remain quite undiminished. In reply to my birthday cable, weeks later, I had a letter wishing me luck in my 'purchased paradise'.

I enjoyed Marseilles. It is a heap of unhypocritical wickedness lying warmly snake-like around some extraordinarily inspiring harbours. The old port where the yachts lie. The new port where the big ships gather. I dragged Alfred Allan around trying to find the Rue Renard. I once tore a print from an edition of the *Saturday Book* of a picture by Edward Wadsworth. It showed women bawling at one another on a street corner. The women had big bosoms, neat black legs, and above them were wonderful ironwork signs advertising rows of brothels. And as through a crack in the houses, looking down on it all, the famous Cathedral of Marseilles, Notre Dame de la Garde, with her huge Christ-child in her arms. There is no Rue Renard any more. It was bombed in the war. But Notre Dame de la Garde is there yet, golden and lovely in the sun.

We climbed the hill to her, partly because whatever country I am in I enjoy sharing in the religious beliefs of that country. Also, Alfred Allan and I had eight hours to kill before the freighter sailed.

The wind up there on the mount, around the cathedral of Our Lady who Guards Us, was truly fierce. I felt that what had been good enough for all those Marseillais for all those centuries was good enough for me, so in we went and on our knees asked for a blessing on our voyage.

Outside the wind howled. It flattened all the people against the cathedral walls: tourists, priests, parents, little children taking their first communion (boys dressed as little white monks, girls as tiny white brides). Inside, everything was still.

The model ships – people had hung them from the ceiling on threads as offerings – scarcely stirred. Around them were homemade galleons three feet high, yachts (exquisite right down to the last detail), fishing craft with beautifully mounted miniature lug sails, all made with love, to scale. There were even models of Cadillacs and aeroplanes hanging there on threads, almost stationary, scarcely swaying. There wasn't a vestige of a draught inside the cathedral.

We blundered back into the sun. And here the wind hit us again. It tore the clouds from the face of the city, it whipped the waves up into a froth, it rocked all the packet boats where they lay at anchor or moored to the mole.

And there, eventually, after a bumpy drive round the tram tracks, our freighter was waiting. Everything seemed lackadaisical indeed. The water-front (in the manner of all water-fronts) was aswarm with highly undesirable characters. 'Leave the Volkswagen here,' they said. 'Leave it unlocked. Go and get some lunch. We don't sail until about two this afternoon.' They spoke in French, and occasionally in bad English. Alfred Allan and I didn't care to go too far away. We drank, in the end, in a tiny water-front café, keeping the Volkswagen under observation until she was swung on board, by crane, high above the crowd of undesirables. Then I went through some sweating moments, parking the Volkswagen on the deck for the bosun. He was a splendid Clark Gable type in a battered peaked cap.

We sailed about four in the afternoon, with an occasional baritone hoot from our funnel.

Tugs eased us away, steadied us, and then let slip their cables. Alfred Allan and I went below to explore our cabins.

Our freighter was a big ship – rebuilt in Glasgow in 1948. It had a splendid hot water system that was guaranteed to hit the most intimate portions of one's anatomy from any angle in the cabin.

There was a splendid first-class saloon and a handful of first-class passengers. Up in the bows there was 'dormitory accommodation', where Arabs crouched with tiny braziers and German Boy Scout types with yellow beards unrolled sleeping bags to doss down on the deck.

Alfred Allan and I inspected these quarters because Bill Taylor (our travel agent in Paris) had originally booked us into them. We were mildly startled. We could see why the Germans were up on deck. The smell of one thing and another was enough to make the hair stand on end. I rather liked the Arabs. They were very dignified in jellabas and djibbahs, with their endless women all shrouded in veiling, who carried the bundles. Suitcases they had obviously never seen. It wouldn't somehow be legal for an Arab wearing a jellaba to own a wife carrying a suitcase.

Down in the hold, which separated us from the Arabs and German hikers, there was a tremendously smelly cargo, mainly of hides and sheepskins and big wooden boxes destined for the Lebanon. We had ample opportunity to look these over as we seemed to load and unload the holds every two days.

We had a most whimsical schedule. We were supposed to put in at Naples. But instead the captain put in at Genoa. There we loaded car after car, rubber tyres, huge packing cases marked: 'Electrical Equipment – Beirut'.

Jonnie and Sheila Van Damm were in Capri and tried vainly to telephone us in Naples. But as our captain ignored his schedule we went sulkily untelephoned, sitting at dinner, Alfred Allan with his soda-water, me with my bottle of retsina, in our first-class dining-room.

The life in the ship was very soothing. We lay on deck all the morning, burning ourselves to a nice crisp red-brown. We lay on deck all the afternoon: ditto. Vaguely, through lowered eyes, we observed 'Clark Gable' bouncing round the Volkswagen. Once, as I watched, he swung lightly on the luggage rack. It came off in his hand. He didn't even look guilty. He tucked it back in place as though nothing had happened.

'Any minute now,' said Alfred Allan, 'your friend Marlene will emerge from those Arab quarters and sing "I Can't Give You Anything But Love, Baby". Or else Jean Harlow. I can't be sure which.'

'Marlene,' I said. 'That's for sure. And she will say "Both of us, schweetheart . . . two of a kind, dwift-wood" to John Wayne.'

'Dwiftwood,' Alfred Allan agreed.

The steady, slow freighter thudded her way south-east, her wake creaming and marbling behind her. Smoothly, silkily, she ironed out my nerves, like a carpenter's plane rasping out rough places in a plank. Around us, occasionally, seagulls screamed after refuse thrown overboard by stewards in white tee-shirts. Overhead the sun shone. Lulled into a false sense of security we went down to the first-class saloon. Always the Muzak on the tape had reached some piece of virtuosity called 'The Grand Canyon Suite' which sent Alfred Allan into hoots of subdued laughter. In spite of our eagerness for Greece we were both sorry when we arrived.

At Piraeus all was chaos. You will recall that Sue Keeble (Harold Keeble's wife) and Rena Harper had decided not to come with us, but had gone off together by some other route. And there on the quay at Piraeus they were standing, unearthly in the dim mauve lights of the quayside.

'Welcome!' they cried, faces milky in the strange light. 'Welcome to Greece!'

SET A THEBES TO CATCH A THEBES

I have read somewhere, almost certainly in a book by John Steinbeck called *Travels with Charley*, that no one can write coherently and honestly about Greece. Something happens, he claims, to romanticise each fact so that the Greek landscape is seen, shimmering slightly, as through a pair of sentimental glasses. Nothing could ever possibly make me sentimentalise about Athens.

Rena's hotel was unprepared for us. Crossly they put us in some rooms that rightly belonged to a Mr and Mrs Wood.

In the morning the desk clerk explained, none too politely, that we had no reservations and must go, and we moved to the Alexiou which had been recommended by Dilys Powell. Halfway there, alas, the Volkswagen stopped. We had run out of petrol. As I had filled the tank the previous day, I simply couldn't believe it. We both peered into the tank. (This was the moment when Alfred Allan dropped in the hunting knife.) The day got hotter and hotter and stickier and stickier as Alfred Allan went to telephone a garage. The garage hated us. They tore up all our free-service booklets for the Volkswagen and when I shrieked and salvaged them, cursing, from the waste-paper basket, they shrugged their shoulders.

Two American tourists, speaking impeccable Greek, helped us out.

'Look, don't despair,' they said. 'They have just decided to give you a bad time, that is all. For some reason.'

One of the young men had a yellow beard and he looked like St. John the Baptist. I liked him. I wished he'd stay and go on interpreting. Because of him we eventually got the Volkswagen on the road again, full of petrol. We decided we would leave Athens *at once*. And on the high road to Thebes the engine stalled again.

I got down from the van. It was pretty hot out there on the highway. I opened the engine, which in a Volkswagen is situated in the rear. Instantly I was covered with oil. Instantly the dust from the road rose and settled on me. Again I cursed, long and fluently. For those men in the garage who, according to St. John, had 'decided to give us a bad time' had disconnected pretty well every bit of tubing that *could* be disconnected. There was petrol flowing all over the road.

'It's the gods,' said Alfred Allan. 'They are against us.'

While I connected tubing Alfred Allan prayed. While I swore and danced as my bare hands encountered bits of red-hot metal, he made his pact with Apollo. Remembering my childhood, I wondered if he would presently sacrifice *me*. But no. He sacrificed himself. Sportingly he said that if only Apollo would apply the light of his reason to the mechanism he, Alfred Allan, would not raise nose from typewriter until his work was done.

'That should fix it,' we both said simultaneously, as I climbed back into the cab beside him. And then our bad temper broke, and we both laughed, as the Volkswagen started with a cough and a spit and we were on the road again.

Across the Attic Plain we went. The heat rose higher and higher. Alfred Allan took off his shirt. He was by now very dark with heat. We peered out at the barren hills, hazy all around us. My tongue was sticking to the roof of my mouth. I have never worked up so monumental a thirst.

In Thebes I parked under some hopeless trees. 'Oedipus Rex,' murmured Allan, eyes tight shut.

We wandered around saying 'ParakaLO' and 'Beer'. The sun whacked down. Flies buzzed. Dogs lay prone. We found a café with three little wobbly chairs. A man dusted one for us. A mangy cat slid by. The sky was dark polished blue.

The beer was cold from the refrigerator. Beaded with cold; our man plonked the bottles down on the table. Glugging, frothing soapily, it emerged into the none-too-clean glasses. Achingly, lovingly, it slid down my throat. I looked at poor Allan, who had sworn to drink soda-water for the trip. He, too, was drinking, swallowing smoothly, greedily.

'Jesu,' he said, with feeling, 'if this is Thebes I don't wonder Oedipus put his eyes out!'

Chapter Four

Countess Drachma

There we sat, out of love with Greece, while the sweat dried again on our faces in a thick, dusty, salty crust and the beer evaporated in my throat. The long road stretched away, filled with mirages, across the plains.

Lafkardia was our next town, the place where the Air France driver had given Granny and me shashlik. Here we were to rendezvous with Rena and Sue Keeble. We drove into it feeling like explorers, looking with joy at trees that held real shade, at the ice cream parlours, the shops selling rugs, postcards, goatskins, horrible little pots with pseudo-Etruscan designs. We parked in the shade and crossed to the biggest ice cream parlour of the lot, where I had more beer, and Alfred Allan had squeezed orange juice and we both had excellent salty, herby shashlik – neat little cubes of lean lamb, spitted on bamboo and scorched in a charcoal grill. We paid. It cost about five shillings. There were plenty of tourists here, for Lafkardia is the place where you turn off the main road for Delphi. Mid-Western voices flattened the atmosphere all around us:

'Oh, isn't this just darling? That saucer is just dee-vyan. Did you see Mrs Schneider's rugs? She's a very lovely person. Delphi is just darling. We are going on by boat. We came by land, but the boat went round by water.'

Having paid our bill, we peacefully relaxed. Then we waited without apprehension for the girls. Tooting, hooting, raising a cloud of dust, they presently came, settled down to eat roughly what we had eaten and *we* were suddenly handed a second bill, this time for £5.

Alfred Allan handed it back politely.

'You are mistaken,' he said. 'I have paid for our lunch and it only cost five shillings.'

He suddenly shot up from his chair, Mr Muscles to the life, and, behaving exactly like the Champ in *Diamond Lil*, he towed me away.

'Where are you going?' asked Rena, reasonably.

'To buy ice cream,' lied Alfred Allan.

'Well, don't buy it there,' said Rena, bossily. 'Look, this is the best shop for ice cream.'

'Countess Drachma,' said Alfred Allan, much to my horror, 'I am a tourist. I *like* being a tourist. I am over twenty-one. I often buy ice cream where I want, and I like doing it. I bought ice cream all alone yesterday and loved it, see?'

And then he towed me away angrily, breathing heavily down his nose. 'Who the hell cares, Allan?' I said. 'What does it matter anyway? Do *relax*.'

Rena and Sue now emerged from the ladies' lavatory,

changed into tight cotton pants and broad-brimmed straw hats. Rena explained that if we didn't drive at seventy miles an hour across the next stretch of country we should miss the ferry from Arkitsa to the island of Euboia and so probably be charged double by the caique men from Skiathos. Drachma by drachma the Greek dream went down the drain, as at a merry clip we followed the dust cloud of Rena and Susan Keeble across the landscape to Atlanti.

'Probably near here that girl ran dropping apples,' growled Alfred Allan. 'Wasn't she called Atlanti, or something? Anyway, there's no danger of *those* girls dropping apples . . . '

Vineyards slid by on either side of the road. The road was sometimes metalled, sometimes not. When it was unmetalled dust flew and settled everywhere, especially on the photographs of *Little Mary Sunshine*. Also, the Volkswagen would leap and clang and lurch through potholes. The day was cooler now. The enemy sun was slowly sliding down towards setting, but it was still fairly hot. In the end I slowed down.

'Better to miss the ferry than to be dead bunnies,' I said to Alfred Allan, in prophetic tones.

Even so, bushes slashed him on his forearms, where he sat with the window open, in the breeze from our progress. Goats lingered ahead of us. Occasionally a mule leapt to get out of our way, and struggled madly at the end of a rope, bells ringing. Shepherds gaped at us. Once or twice we slammed through a village street where crooked signs on rusty tin said 'Fery Boat' with one 'r'. Then Rena's dust still hung there, scintillating, and chickens still flew squawking from her progress.

Eventually we arrived at Arkitsa on a beach of shingle that was still sun-warmed. The lazy sea lapped blue-green and clean beyond a tide mark of weed. Hot, dusty, my one wish was to dive into that sea.

'What about the ferry?' asked Alfred Allan.

'I was wrong about that,' said Rena, cheerfully, sunning herself on the steps of a tiny restaurant in her bikini. 'There won't be another ferry for an hour –'

'You mean we needn't have *hurried* –' began Alfred Allan, in his steady, shouting voice.

'Oh, shut *up*,' I hissed. 'Get into your trunks and swim . . .'

And we changed, giggling slightly, inside the hot Volkswagen. It was like an oven after Thebes, after Lafkardia, after the Attic Plain.

But the long, cool, silky embrace of the sea restored everything. Even Alfred Allan began to laugh, throwing drops of water from his head, shaking all over like a dog with pleasure. I dived down through unmatched depths and picked up golden pebbles and as the salt began to sting my eyes all dust and flies and drachma arguments were washed away. In the sea at Atlanti my Greek dream returned.

AEDIPSOS MANIACS

After swimming, salt sinking slowly into my skin, munching digestive biscuits, I watched the ferry boat approaching across the water. The ferry boat was huge and clean and painted white on the superstructure. It was a converted landing craft and it had a little bar with ice and beer and ouzo. There was room in its jaws for buses, cars, lorries, bicycles and trucks. Some of the trucks had wallpaper and velvet curtains, and many of them had pictures of saints, framed in tinsel, or the Sacred Heart hanging round the driving seat.

On the upper deck were wooden benches where we would lie out flat. And when we reached Aedipsos the ferry let down its ponderous iron jaws again and spewed forth trucks, buses, cars and people, like a dragon. We scarcely saw Aedipsos, because the dusk was gone. It was full darkness as we followed Rena's headlights along the shore road to Orei.

A huge Greek moon rose like a silver dollar. Then there was a burst of music and bright light and dancing people and we were in Orei. Hours late, I gather. There two caiques patiently waited, slopping about by the quayside.

Nobody seemed angry that we had kept them waiting. We all instantly became dear old pals. Bottles of iced brandy were handed round, from one to another. We drank deeply. Alfred Allan sadly sipped his soda. A tall fair Swedish-looking man called Stanislas Gunter introduced himself and his wife, who was very British indeed. Skippers shook hands. Car headlights were turned full on the caiques and I inched the Volkswagen on board along two narrow planks. Stas Gunter refused to do this with his Sunbeam Alpine, but he was the only person who seemed to think the procedure was dangerous.

Finally we sailed. We lay on the after deck, wrapped in a sail. On we chugged into the moon track, across the black water, which slid by, trembling in phosphorescence. We sailed slowly, our mast etching a pattern against the moon.

I slept. I dreamed of nothing. When I woke Rena was shaking me by the arm. We were passing a tiny island with a winking light on top of it. Behind there was the bulk of Skiathos. My land again, for the second time. On it, perhaps there might be a house. The shell of a house. It was too dark to see.

Chapter Five

Holiday Camp

I woke for two minutes stumbling along the quay, past the petrol station to an hotel. Here a yawning girl put pillow-slips on pillows. I looked at my watch. I think it was around 4 a.m. Then I slept again, until the sun, unshaded, woke me with a blow between the eyes. Also, someone was speaking Greek. I dimly understood them to say that they wanted the Volkswagen off the caique. How could I know what anyone said at seven in the morning? Seven? Was I kidding? It *was five* . . .

Rubbing sleep from my eyes, I went down on the quay. Gus Merodes was there. We shook hands, delightedly. Under his directions, I drove the Volkswagen off. It took no time at all.

I went to the café and sat down outside it. It was the same proprietor who had served Granny and me. I had seen him in an advertising film. He was delighted. He poured me a cup of Turkish coffee and some iced water. Rena came by. She drove *her* car off the caique.

'What do you want to do?' she asked, obligingly.

'I want to see my house,' I said.

'I'm afraid you won't be able to camp too near,' she said. 'You see the General's Road isn't finished and only a goat could get up there. Well, obviously we can walk up there. But you can't take your caravan.'

Alfred Allan appeared, strolling thoughtfully along the quay. When he saw Rena he bowed. She bowed back.

'The road isn't ready up to the house,' I began. 'So–'

'Road not ready up to the house?' Alfred Allan shouted, unwaveringly. 'What have we come all this way for, then, if we can't drive near to your house?'

'What would you like?' Rena asked. 'A lovely beach? Where you can swim . . . ?'

'We'll need water there,' I said. 'Fresh water. Yes, a beach, for camping. But don't worry, Rena, we'll easily find something.'

'The road will be ready the next time you come,' said Rena, placatingly. 'And meanwhile I'll show you a really lovely beach, owned by sweet people, friends of mine. What have you got there?'

'Eggs,' I said. 'Eggs. I bought them from the café.'

'Well, these people will have plenty of eggs. Look. You had better get to the camp at once. Sue Keeble and I will bring the things you need, like ice and so on, later. Do you want a cup of coffee?' she asked Alfred Allan.

He reeled back from the sweet Turkish mud, which I was drinking quite happily. 'No, thank you,' said Allan, politely. 'I'll wait until we get into camp.'

And then the usual helter-skelter chase of Rena began, along the island road.

To begin with this wound through impossibly narrow paved streets, where mules strutted, children sat sucking their thumbs, and women sat sideways on little donkeys, spinning yarn on to spindles. Olive trees began, and vineyards and pine trees. There were tiny wounds in the pine trees, with tin buckets hanging below them, to catch the resin. Then the road began to climb steeply. We shot through the Army Camp, where the Captain had stood. Now nobody was stirring in the camouflaged bell tents. Then we burst out by the cliffs. We looked down on the left-hand side, some sheer forty feet to the sea.

Rena had stopped.

'What's she stopping for?' Alan asked.

'It's her house, I think,' I replied. And so it was. It was almost finished. Swarms of men, excitedly plastering, were buzzing around like ants. Across the bay I now saw something. My house. I tried to focus my eyes through the heat haze across the bay. Pink. It was *pink*. Why weren't the builders doing anything to it?

'Something to do with drachmai,' Allan murmured, standing huge, gloomy, hands deep in the pockets of his cotton trousers, feet in dirty sneakers, rolling a stone or two down the path to the sea, a raincoat turned up to his ears. 'It is lovely, though.'

'Do you want to go to your house now?' Rena asked me.

'No,' I said, swallowing my depression. 'Look, let's see it tomorrow. Where's this beautiful beach?'

Rena left her house. The road wound on through olive groves, dotted here and there with little square boxes of houses. Then we came to a broad and pleasant valley. There seemed to be watermelons growing. A rough track led down to the sea, to a beach so golden that the word 'golden' cannot do it justice.

By the beach, under pine trees, stood a little farm. A pig-sty, a hen house, a cottage. All very primitive. And a family. Pa, Ma and a baby boy of about four years old. They welcomed Rena shyly. They helped us stow the Volkswagen under a pine tree on the shifting sand. Rena waved goodbye. We put the coffee on the stove. We felt slightly more human.

Allan got out his typewriter and set it up in the living-room of the caravan, on the table.

'Must keep my word to Apollo,' he said cheerfully.

The sea called insistently, whispering on the warm sand. I unpacked the Pouilly Fumé, remembering romantic stories of cooling things in the sea. Vain thought. The sea was well into the eighties. Pa arrived back from the village with his mule laden down with ice. I packed it into our ice box and put the wine in again. And still the temperature rose.

By about half past one, when the beach was grilling nicely, and Alfred Allan and I had been in and out of the sea a few times, the party arrived. There was Susan Keeble and Stanislas Gunter and his wife, and Rena and two young Greek soldiers. They all flung off their clothes and flung themselves into the sea.

When they emerged I entertained them as best I could, handing round digestive biscuits and finishing off the last of the curdled Pouilly Fumé on them. Then they left, and the silence of the place slipped back around my ears.

I followed them to the cars, to speed them on their way.

'Oh,' I said, 'and you must excuse Allan. He has come here to work and think and I hate to interrupt him.'

Now and hereafter I used the unfortunate Alfred Allan as an excuse to prolong my silence. Nina and Frederik have a song that might have been written for that beach:

> 'The silence of noon
> The clamour of night
> The heat of the day
> When the fish won't bite . . .'

The words, the music, beat incessantly in my ears. I thanked God that I had acquired a protective tan on the ship, for the sun was fiercer than anything I had ever known. And I was already hypnotised by another island about half a mile out, on our immediate horizon.

It was well into the afternoon; the sun was cooling a little when I started to swim. I had not got over my disappointment about the house. I wanted to see it immediately, now, make plans about it. But it was at least three miles away, and in this heat I wasn't going to start out walking back along *that* road. Instead I slid along in that warm sea, with all the speed of a dolphin, a flying fish.

Every now and then I would dive. I was able to see, ignoring the smarting of my eyelids, at least fifteen feet down into a city of seaweed, rock, sea urchin, patches of amethyst, lapis lazuli, turquoise, sapphire depths. And the shadows subtly changed as I passed over and through them, clearly outlined on the rocks below.

And then I reached the tiny island.

It was a small paradise of green bushes, lavender, pine trees sown by the wind. I lay out there, among the rocks. I scraped up a sea urchin, got it somehow in two and scooped it out. It tasted salty and sweet, delicious.

Far away I could see Alfred Allan stretching himself, walking about, thinking, down at the water's edge. Alfred Allan's mother lives in Brooklyn and is often asked by the neighbours what her son is doing. 'My son, the writer, is thinking,' she replies, proudly.

Well, I could see him thinking now. A gust of wind came from nowhere and scattered his script in the shadows. He ran, picking up pages. I was too far away, too drowsy to help him. 'My thinker, the son, is writing,' I murmured to myself. 'My writer, the thinker, is sunning.' And then I fell heavily asleep in the shade of the tiny pine trees on the island.

When I woke the sun was setting, and I slid into the sea and swam back to the beach, back to supper and some of our reconstituted supermarket soup. The kitchen of the caravan worked perfectly, but neither of us could bear to be indoors. So we sat outside.

When the sun went down the stars scattered the sky in

vulgar profusion. The moon extracted the colour from everything, from the land, from our faces.

Pa came from his little house with a lantern to hang on our tree – instantly moths, mosquitoes, flying ants would descend. So I handed it back to Pa, saying, 'No, no please' (*Oichi Oichi parakalo*), and a bewildered Pa returned to his house. I noticed he too slept out of doors. He quickly dossed down on his veranda in a sort of blanket. And so did we. We heaved the mattress out of the caravan for me. We blew up the Lilo for Alfred Allan.

And there we lay, cheerfully counting stars, on the open beach. When I was sick of counting stars I counted night noises. Once I counted about one hundred and seventy before I slid to oblivion. Mule bells, mule teeth tearing grass, hens clucking softly, pigs splashing, child crying, cricket twittering, man singing, wind sighing, sea rustling . . .

'Do you see that light up there?' Alfred Allan suddenly asked.

'What light?'

I sat up. I was rather cross at being disturbed. Far overhead, at enormous speed, a light was going by.

'It isn't an aeroplane, it isn't making any noise,' said Alfred Allan.

'It must be one of those sputniks,' I remarked vaguely.

'We'll never know,' said Alfred Allan. 'Perhaps it is Russian. Who cares . . .'

And we both slept, deeply. The next week Alfred

Allan had a letter from his mother which explained it all. It must have been Scott Carpenter in Mercury 7.

IT NEVER DRAINS IN EDEN

How long was I on the island that time? Alfred Allan says, without bitterness, a long weekend.

'A lawng way to come for a lawng weekend,' he often says, when he wants to upset me. It is true, I expect, for I have no more idea what day it was than what time it was. I don't know if we arrived on a Thursday or a Friday, and if we did what we did with these days.

Perhaps, in any case, for the sake of Alfred Allan's health it was just as well it only was a long weekend. For we would both wake each morning, completely stiff. Then Alfred Allan would knock the coffee-pot over, or spill the grounds into the scrambled eggs. And I would disappear into the bushes with my spade. All this happened at sun-up, at about 4 a.m., because Pa used to drive his mules, skipping friskily along the beach, to water at that time.

I am quite uninhibited and have never minded this sort of thing. But Alfred Allan never went at all.

One night there was singing and mollocking in a house up the hill, so I supposed it was Saturday. I was rather afraid of the mollocking Greeks, and lay with *the* spade ready to hand beside me. And one morning Rena came with her car to drive me over to look at my house.

Nowadays the General's Road runs right to my front door, and there is even a space in which I can park. But in those days we had to leave the car and walk through somebody else's farm and across somebody else's meadows to get there. (Even now a dog dashes from the farm, barking furiously, whenever I drive by.)

Tethered goats seemed to be everywhere, and as we passed them they sprang in the air, ran wildly away and crashed heavily at the end of their tethers, helpless and terrified. Then they would get up and do it all over again. I never saw anything so restless. You would think even a goat would learn.

And there finally stood the beginnings of my poor little house unloved, neglected and dishevelled, perched precariously on the edge of the cliff. Half-bricks lay everywhere. The corners were ragged and unfinished. Rafters and beams, half planed, stuck out at all angles. Everything was dusty. A half-can of turpentine lay on its side, with an old rag. Torn and dirty paper lay all around the house in the bushes.

As I gazed and gazed, Rena waved her arms about and said how beautiful the view was from each of the windows.

'How about my well?' I asked.

Rena started to explain. Something to do with the old gent (whom I had seen down among the goats in the meadows). He had waved cheerfully and I had cried out 'Gazoo! Gazoo!' (Whatever the hell *this* means – I *hope* it means 'comrade'.)

'He wants to be paid if you dig in his land, but I won't have that,' said Rena.

And she said how beautiful the view was. It *was* beautiful, too, but I felt an awful impulse come over me to quote the story of Sir John Gielgud at her. Sir John, having climbed the great cliff path at Portofino and been told by his hostess (Lilli Palmer) to look at the view, replied firmly, 'I just don't like it . . . I just don't like it.'

It wouldn't have been true, of course. I did like it, oh how I liked it! But one does *not* like one's romantic island illusions shattered by sordid details like money. Money for builders. For plumbers. For carpenters. For a series of people with whom you can't communicate or argue. Who will build what they please, when they please, and only if they please. And then charge you any sum they please.

Rena was doing her very best, but sometimes I suspect she found me even more odd and difficult and eccentric than the workmen. But throughout she kept her temper, and beamed at us all, and when in doubt she said, so rightly, how beautiful the view was. I am not always very practical. But I did grasp the fact that everybody wanted to be paid.

'I shall have to go back to work,' I explained, 'and write a book to make some money to pay the builders. I also think I shall have to take the advice of an architect.

'Right now,' I went on, 'I am going to spend what money I have here on my holiday. But when I get back to England I shall send some more.'

She drove me back to Alfred Allan and our holiday camp. She also handed over the mail.

Alfred Allan was battering away at his typewriter. So I sat down on the sand and read my letters. I was already very depressed.

The first letter was from Jonnie, care of the mayor of Skiathos. A nice touch, I thought. It said, despairingly, that Nicky, her beloved elder son, had blown himself up in the chemistry lab and might even lose the use of a hand. The second was from the *News of the World*, asking for a column immediately. The third was from Granny saying that if I came back *at once* I might be able to do something for *Little Mary Sunshine*. 'It needs you for the publicity, otherwise . . .'

And at this very moment the wind rose. I had heard tales of the mistral in the Greek islands: of how once it really blows around the islands of Skópelos and Skiathos particularly, that channel of sea is virtually impassable. The wind was hot and dry and fearsome. As the saying is: 'It was enough to drive a man mad.'

I didn't, at first, share my terrible depression with Alfred Allan.

I swam instead, trying to get out of the wind. But the sea had gone cold. I crouched behind rocks. I crouched in the olive grove. I tried to take refuge on little beaches surrounded with natural windbreaks, fig trees and so on. The ants came and looked at me. They seemed big as bulldogs. I put my clothes on and walked for miles along the road, almost as far as my house. I was accosted by peasant women who patted my stomach and asked, 'Baby?' I shook my head and said, 'Next year, maybe,' craftily. Finally, unable to stand it a moment longer, I returned to Alfred Allan and said, with drama:

'We must go. I can't stand it, I can't stand it – this terrible wind!'

Alfred Allan seemed only mildly surprised. And this was the first occasion that he said, 'It seems a helluva lawng way to come for a lawng weekend.'

Chapter Six

Vo-ee-the-AY! Vo-ee-the-AY!

That, to tell the truth, was that. No matter how hard one may try to prolong an adventure, when the adventure is over, it is over. The savage thrusts with which the pen writes 'Finis' at the end of a love affair wrote 'Finis' then and there on the beach.

I had, of course, until my peaceful little universe cracked, had four days of Eden. Hundreds of people have never had so much. I had sat under my pine tree through the white heat of the day, feeling the sun bite through the narrow leaves into my flesh. I had hobbled across sand so hot that it seemed to blister my feet. I had loved it.

I used to go to the well just after sunrise. I trod daintily along a sun-baked crumbling path between the water-melons, lowered my canvas bucket into cool depths where flies buzzed and baby ferns grew, daintily. When Ma discovered that I was going to the well (Alfred Allan and I agreed right from the start that water-carrying was woman's work in Greece and when I was in Greece I would do as the Greeks did) she used to dash to get in there first. She got up earlier and earlier so that she could cheat me to the bucket.

Once the baby boy woke when Ma was out at the well.

He burst out of the house, sobbing his anger and dismay. I was the nearest female human, and I seized him, hugging him closely, murmuring good English noises like, 'There, there, then, good, good bunny then, Mummy's at the well.' I also pointed (in Greek) across at the well where Ma, her head already wrapped in rags against the enemy sun, was cheerfully plodding home, a bucket in either hand.

Once his eyes had focused on Ma I put him down. He scampered to her through the fields in his little cotton pyjamas. When he reached her she put the buckets down. And then he was hugged even more closely, even more reassuringly. After this Alfred Allan and I tried to talk to him. It was hopeless. He was too shy. He would run to Mummy's skirts and hide there, giggling. He had no toys. He had never seen a toy. When we gave him a tin can with a pebble in it he was overjoyed, although we had to show him how to rattle it. By the standards of Western civilisation that child had nothing at all. Except, of course, the universe. He had the undivided attention and love of Ma, who fairly ate him up. He was the most utterly spoiled child I have ever seen. Now he has a sister, and there is another baby on the way; so even his sister's reign will be short. Now he is father's boy and rides high on the crupper of father's white plough-horse. Soon he will be bent double in the fields with a wife of his own and a little boy of his own. It is unlikely that he will leave his Eden. When the island people leave, even for the USA, they soon come back and marry island girls.

But that afternoon when the mistral, or the sirocco, or whatever they call that hellish hot wind, hit us, the beach no longer seemed like Eden. As the sand rose in great swirling gusts and stung my cheeks and bent the pine tree double, it actually seemed like hell. Alfred Allan and Sue Keeble and I and Ma tried to get the Volkswagen off the sand.

The sand, which had supported our weight without protest while we remained stationary, positively refused to take the bite and drive of the wheels when the engine was revved up.

We sank, and sank, and sank, wheels spinning furiously right up to the axles, while Ma and Allan and Sue threw mats and bits of old carpet and terrible pieces of splintered wood under the whirling tyres. I was sure we would puncture them. I cursed and swore.

'You do look funny,' said Alfred Allan. 'You're grey all over, even your hair.'

If grey hair was all I had from this episode I would be lucky. I said so, and stopped, exhausted and beaten. And then Alfred Allan's great loud voice, like a bull-frog bellowing, came into its own at last. Also, the Greek vocabulary which we had learned from Dilys all those months ago at rehearsals of *My Word!* Away on the General's Road we could see the Army, gently driving the bulldozer back to its kennel after a day of road making.

'VO-EE-the-AY! VO-EE-the-AY!' (help . . . help), cried Allan unwaveringly.

The bulldozer swung off the road towards us. The Greek god driving it attached a steel cable to the bumper of the Volkswagen. And pulled. The bumper came off, as neatly as you please, just like the wing off a fly. The Greek god grinned. Then he attached the cable to the axle. (My mind began arguing insurance claims. To one back axle . . . to one bumper . . . well, you see how it was, m'lud). Then he went, shudderingly, into reverse. There was a terrible sucking noise. Out flew the Volkswagen, moaning and twitching, exactly like a cow rescued from a bog. Sand flew everywhere. Grinning broadly, the Greek god now pulled us clear of the beach, into the middle of the water-melons to the rough meadow track. And there he posed for his photograph with Pa and Ma and the baby boy. And then he drove away to Skiathos port, laughing heartily.

We kissed Ma. We shook hands with Pa. The boy wouldn't let us kiss him. He hid, as usual, giggling, in Ma's skirts. We gave Ma all our packets of dried soup – she and two other ladies used to hang around the doorway of the Volkswagen kitchen in the evening when I was making soup for *Kyrius* (mister) – all our tinned soup, a tin-opener and a great big slice of my heart. It took ages to teach her how to use the tin-opener. She had never seen anything like it. We also tried to give her money. We had an awful struggle making her accept anything at all, but in the end she took a very little.

And then, with sweat making runnels down my dusty face and my gritty body, Alfred Allan and I drove back to the port and hired a caique from Gus Merodes to take us off in the morning. I spent a wild and foolish night, telling the fortunes of German tourists (in German), and in the morning, Eden being truly dissipated, we sailed back to the mainland through the roughest sea I have ever seen on that coast. We were the only vessel to sail that day, from Skiathos, Skópelos or Volos. We felt, as we tossed this way and that, as the Volkswagen overhung the waves first one way, and then the other, extremely odd. It was an exhilarating crossing, to say the least of it. And neither of us felt even mildly sick.

Back in Paris, after the primitive stresses of our beach-combing life, everyone seemed to be in exactly the same position. Marlene was still telling that great story which begins, 'And I said to him, "*Si j'étais putain*, schweet-heart",' and doing a remarkably funny imitation of Melina Mercouri and Anthony Perkins in *Phaedra*. And, because I was deep in sun-tan and Greek sandals, she heralded all my entrances with, 'Oh hell . . . and here comes another Phaedra.' That put me, and all that Marlene now referred to as 'The Gweek Bit', in its place.

And Alfred Allan and I attended a birthday party, given for him by two nice Americans, Jack and Gurney Campbell, in their house in Montparnasse, somewhere near the statue of the Lion of Belfort. Hundreds of guests were there, in dinner-jackets and long evening gowns. A platform had been built on the grass and musicians played under a striped marquee. Everyone danced the twist. The excellent novelist, Muriel Spark, in green satin and long tan gloves, drank champagne with a lady in a petunia Balenciaga evening gown, dangling with the Legion of Honour.

All around us, looking upwards and outwards, were the working-class homes of the working-class people of Paris. As we cavorted, feeling like something perfectly splendid from Ol' Virginny, there was an effect of magnolia in the air.

Then the windows of Montparnasse flew up. And tomatoes and ripe fruit and eggs came shooting down. They missed me. They missed Alfred Allan by inches. But they struck Miss Muriel Spark a heavy smack upon her elegant green satin bosom.

It was then that I realised that I was not alone in thinking the Right Bank Parisian existence a somewhat empty and trivial one.

WHICH WENT FIRST, RUTTERFORD OR THE CHICKEN?

I left Paris at 4 a.m. that day, feeling as though the adventure was beginning again. I could see that I must return to Skiathos as soon as possible: but how, and when, and where should I get the money? And, anyway, what was the point until I had finished the house? I was obsessed by the recollections of that gallant shell, half finished, sitting there in mute appeal on the top of its cliff. Terraces needed to be built down to the water's edge. The builder would have to be paid. And what about the plumber? And what about the *drains*?

Back in London I agreed to accept a lecture tour through America. The sum I expected to make there (about £500) wouldn't complicate my English tax situation too badly and I would be able to send the money directly to the plumber and/or the builder. And with a mortgage to pay off on a new London house I wouldn't feel that I was immoral by exploiting Spain and Laurie (Exploitation) Ltd. over a house and a project for which so far Jonnie expressed only a weary dismay.

So to America I went. And my American experiences, wild and glorious though they were, will form no part of this narrative. My love for America forms another book, which I may one day write.

So there I was in London, faced with the long, damp, dog days of summer. I was tormented by my recollections of the island. It called insistently to me, as though it had put me under a spell.

And, more practical, the report from that sweet architect Doxiadis now arrived. When we read it together my good friend Roy Rutterford promptly volunteered to go and see if he could help Doxiadis' recommendations to be put into effect.

Doxiadis' report was perfectly splendid.* It had phrases

* See Appendix, page 267.

in it of great and lasting joy. If this is the sort of thing you like (it said, in effect), then this is the sort of thing you like. The house is sound. And, by George, there is actually a drainage system. I had a cesspit, where the seepage was slightly rum but adequate. And there was a tank on the roof, to be filled from petrol cans (after the custom of the country) by a man on a mule. 'Again,' said the report, apparently only mildly disgusted, 'this system is considered perfectly adequate in this part of Greece.'

Rutterford and I pored over the report. Unless you have been concentrating like a crazy mad thing you will not remember who he is. He is the friend who once on page 99 of this book drove me through North Africa to the Pillars of Hercules so that I could swim in the Atlantic.

Rutterford is of medium height. He is very strong, very tanned and very practical. In his day, in addition to running hotels in Goa and Tangier, he has been a merchant seaman, an editor, an advertising man (both on TV and in magazines), and he has converted boats and villas. He has a flair for interior decoration, and he now owns a dashing restaurant called 'The Eyebrow' in Fulham.

I sold this, I raked together that, I interviewed my long-suffering bank manager, and Rutterford set out, with a new set of tyres (part of the deal) and a very temperamental companion indeed, for Skiathos.

He refused to go by freighter. Said it was far too expensive. He refused to drive through Italy and take the

Brindisi–Patras ferry. Too expensive. He would (he said) tackle the route through Yugoslavia.

He then seemed to disappear from the face of the earth. I heard nothing at all for at least a month, then one day suddenly had a wire: 'CAN SELL WHOLE THING AT COST – RUTTERFORD.' I was furious. I cabled back don't be idiotic, get on with the bloody job, and nothing more was heard of Rutterford or his friend. Then one day I suddenly had a telephone call from him from the South of France, and I recognised that he had been a victim of an island panic as strong as my own.

Eventually he turned up in London and tried to tell Jonnie and me what had gone on. He was mildly incoherent. But after a lot of piecing together, I gathered that Skiathos hadn't been the Garden of Eden for him at all.

'I arrived at the height of the season,' he said. 'It was *terribly* hot. The only room left in the place was in the port, and I had to share it with a chicken, tethered to the tap. One day I came down and found the chicken flat on its back with its claws in the air, and I said, "By God, what's too much for the bloody chicken is too much for me, too," and I got the hell out. And here I am.'

And he went off into peals of merry laughter.

With some ceremony we awarded Rutterford the Order of Skiathos with Crossed Palms.

And then, as we sat there, drinking cups of tea and looking at plans and drawings of the house in the kitchen, a telegram arrived from Rena:

'PLUMBER WILL DO INSTALLATIONS OF BATH ETC IN RETURN FOR A LEATHER JACKET,' it said.

My God,' said Rutterford. 'Do you suppose she means the insect?'

Chapter Seven

A Jacket for the Plumber

Even Rutterford agreed that the island was the most beautiful place he had ever seen. He said he thought that if he went back there with someone with a sense of humour who could laugh at everything, probably he would enjoy it very much. He had made the mistake, in my opinion, of thinking in somewhat preconceived terms. He had left his car on the mainland, because caiques were too expensive, and so left himself helpless without transport on the island.

'I thought I could always hire a mule, you see,' he said. 'That's where I made my foolish mistake. All the mules were working hard, and nobody could understand me when I said I wanted to hire one.'

In fact, although he mocked himself, Rutterford had achieved a very great deal. Under his supervision tiles had somehow been selected and laid down, so that one could wash the whole villa floor all through. A wall had been knocked down, and rebuilt so that I had a small private study in between the living-room and the master bedroom. The study was quite big enough to work in *and* sleep in, and there was room for a small cupboard for clothes behind the door. Rena, with Roy's co-operation, had been able to start the builders working again, and this time was keeping them hard at it. Everything suddenly seemed like the Garden of Eden once again. Perhaps the house *would* be ready by May next year.

I must say, when I walked through its half-finished walls, and contemplated the slit that would one day be the kitchen, and looked at the second-best bedroom which would one day take the heat of the sun from the best bedroom, the study and the living-room, it had all seemed to me considerably more chaotic than the original green cliff-top jungle.

But now, with Rutterford sitting there with his plans and drawings, there even began to be a likelihood of furniture getting into the place one day.

'How about the *road*?' I asked, remembering something. 'Have they built the General's Road so that it runs by the door, or do you walk up through all those hen-runs, and goats and things?'

Rutterford stared. He had done so much else. He had forgotten how he had got there. I began to wonder if he had actually been. (This is the awful effect of the island of Skiathos. Everyone begins to doubt everyone in time. It is as though the place were enchanted.)

'Did you walk?' I repeated, as Rutterford's honest if somewhat battered face struggled with the efforts of recollection.

'Rena drove me there in her car,' he said, finally. 'I

think. Once I went by boat. That was when I took these photographs.'

'But did you drive up to the door? Or did you *walk*?' I realised my voice was rising, shrill with the frustrations of being fifteen hundred miles away from the place. 'I mean, dear,' I went on, in more normal tones, 'will we ever be able to deliver *furniture* by road at all? Or shall we have to take the stove and the fridge and things across by boat?'

Rutterford shook his head.

'At the moment I suppose by sea would be best. So few people have cars. Of course, one could . . .'

'. . . always get a mule,' I finished. And we both burst out laughing.

That winter in England surpassed all previous efforts at horror. For months we lay under a thick grey-white blanket of snow and ice and fog, roughly from 29th December until the end of March. At some point in the spring, when ice still lay around, grimed and blackened with disuse, my mother had an operation for cataracts. Within the family we all began to communicate more than usual. I discovered, for example, that my sister Liz had spent the previous summer in Greece, at Corfu and Hydra and Delphi, at roughly the same time (I think) as Alfred Allan and myself, and she too had fallen in love with Greece. She longed, longed, longed to go back. Her husband hated it. Too hot. Too much driving. Perhaps we could go together?

My sister Liz is an enchanting woman of enormous chic

and ability. At the age of eighteen, gripping a Diploma in Design from the Royal College of Art, she plunged into and endured hideous adventures of one sort and another in the wholesale dress business, ending up with great spirit and verve, making a huge success of a factory of her own in Cork, Ireland. Her heart and soul (which had always been those of an artist) were untouched by any of the sordid and bizarre things and people she encountered along the way, and hope undiminished, as I write, she has plunged back into the business again. Good luck to her. It is already a huge success, at 41 Lowndes Square, where you will find it under the name of 'Liza Spain'.

So far as clothes and fashion are concerned her reactions have always been extreme and violent. She would not have been a success in her profession as a designer were this not so. It is disconcerting, to say the least, if you do not share my sister's passion and enthusiasm, to hear a hem or the insert of a sleeve discussed as if it were a defaulting Cabinet Minister or a painting by El Greco.

She is beautiful, my sister Liz, and her way of life has made of her a work of art. Her nails, for example, are always long and beautifully polished. Her hair always shines, burnished like that of a little girl brushed by Nanny for the party. She has a high, light speaking voice, huge short-sighted hazel eyes and a manner of extreme inconsequence which hides a will of steel.

I have, in fact, often written about her before. In the days when I had not yet become a journalist and general columnist I used to write detective stories. The heroine of these was a ballerina named Natasha and based upon my sister Liz. There were eight or nine of these episodes, at least one of which, *Cinderella Goes to the Morgue*, I wrote in Ireland, in my sister's factory, with my sister peering over my shoulder in the evening to read what I had written during the day. Another book, *Not Wanted on Voyage*, foretold with uncanny accuracy Natasha's marrying a charming baronet called Sir Timothy Shelley who was almost exactly like her present husband. Everything, even the Rag Trade, has always been a little bit fey seen through my sister's eyes. Somewhat like the island of Skiathos, there always seems to be a degree of charming going on . . .

Through the truly frightening ice and snow and fog of the English winter, which left me both yellow and shaking with fatigue, I had little time to 'discuss' the Greek trip with sister Liz.

I am so used to being ordered to foreign parts at a moment's notice, and I travel with so little luggage, and I pay so little attention to my personal appearance anyway, that I am always intolerant of the enormous amount of baggage needed by proper ladies when *they* travel. The overnight make-up case, the endless layers of tissue paper: these are absolute necessities for the Proper Lady. I know it. I have seen Claudette Colbert packing to go here and there. And very impressive she is, too, and she arrives the other end as neat as ninepence, with never a crease across the lap of her skirt, nor a rumple in the satin evening coat. Such apparently artless simplicity and perfection is achieved only by a hell of a lot of hard work, believe me.

As May came nearer, my sister Liz would sometimes ring up, asking plaintively for a discussion about luggage. I was truly nonplussed. I was beating round Lancashire, Cheshire, Yorkshire and points north, in all that snow, talking to the women's clubs of England, and getting ready to nurse Mamma through the fortnight's convalescence that would follow her operation. Luggage? I couldn't quite see what we would discuss.

'Bring what you find necessary,' I finally said. 'The Hillman has a big boot. I shall have things for the house in the back of the car, but at a pinch we could get a suitcase or two in there. It would mean we wouldn't be able to open the hood of course.'

'Oh my God, in all that sun I couldn't have the hood down,' cried my sister. 'I have a very delicate skin.'

'Bring whatever you like,' I said. 'There's room for at least three suitcases each if you like.'

'Oh, I don't think I need *three* suitcases,' said sister Liz, far away on the telephone in the middle of Hampshire. But her voice sounded faint with disappointment. I know now that she wanted to *discuss* . . .

Finally matters reached a little climax. We were able to get together for roughly a quarter of an hour in sister Liz's bedroom at the Hyde Park Hotel. All this was my fault. I was seldom in London, and when I was I was always dashing wildly between TV studio and newspaper office. Sister Liz, too, had her problems. As she was then about to go back into business, she, too, was preoccupied with interviewing prospective mannequins, receptionists and so on. Controlling her irritation with me most nobly, she managed to ask a few questions:

'Are there cupboards to hang clothes in?'

(I realised there were no cupboards to hang *anything* in.)

'What is it like exactly?'

(I realised, judging by Rutterford's incoherence, that it was probably changing all the time.)

'If I don't like it may I leave?'

My answers, to say the least of it, were unsatisfactory.

'It is the most beautiful place I have ever seen. But primitive.' That was hardly a help. 'If the house is not ready we can stay in an hotel down in the port but I wouldn't care to. Rena is very kind and anxious for us to stay with her. Yes, of course you can leave if you don't like it. I realise you need a proper holiday.' In the back of my mind I heard Alfred Allan's drawling voice, 'It's a helluva *lawng* way to go even for a *lawng* weekend.'

With variations we went around these points.

'I don't know,' sister Liz would say, from time to time, tapping on things with a pencil with which she had been trying to take notes and make all business-like, 'it all sounds different from when we talked last, somehow. I don't know.'

As sisters will, when faced with the sudden incontrovertible fact that, although evidently of the same flesh and blood, this flesh and blood has been arranged in a totally dissimilar fashion, our voices began to rise in key, and to break. Finally my sister Liz said: 'You're very tired. You'd better go to bed.'

And I went, thoroughly ashamed of myself. As usual, I realised in retrospect I had been defending my relation-ship with the island of Skiathos as though I were having a disreputable love affair with it.

In the morning things looked more hopeful. Sister Liz and I spoke on the telephone. We agreed that everything would be all right if we didn't lose our sense of humour *simultaneously*.

I sent poor Rena a series of cables asking her (a) to construct cupboards and (b) to book us into an hotel in the port. Then I started to make lists of my own of what I thought the house needed.

Kenneth Harper now came to London and I conferred with him about the cupboards. Yes, he was sure they could be built in time and obviously I would need them one day. But before then there were other, more vital, things. 'For example,' he said, mildly, 'I think you should have glass in your windows, don't you? Of course, there are shutters, and they can be closed against the weather, but I think you should have glass in the windows when you are living there.'

My jaw slowly dropped. I dumbly nodded. Eventually I managed to speak.

'How much will the glass cost, would you think?' I asked.

I realised, and not for the first time, how utterly insular

my ideas were. A house with windows, but no glass in them. Well, imagine that. I wonder what sister Liz would have said if she had been a witness to this conversation. I never dared to let her know this further manifestation of the glory that is Greece. I sat down to write to Rena for the hundredth time, knowing that I now faced plumbers' bills, carpenters' bills *and* glaziers' bills.

Suddenly Rena, too, turned up in England. She was really the one with whom my sister Liz should have 'discussed'. How about cupboards? I asked her. It was vital that my sister should have cupboards to put things in . . .

'Well,' explained Rena, 'they have built me very good cupboards. Your house is exactly the same shape as mine. I dare say they can exactly reproduce my cupboards, if they will do?'

Of course they would. Not for the first time I thanked Rena effusively, with tears in my eyes, and for a moment or two I stopped worrying about the cupboards. I handed over the leather jacket, which I had promised the plumber. Rena looked at it and shook her head.

'I have promised proper leather,' she said.

Again my jaw dropped. 'Tiny' Lear, the then deputy editor of the *News of the World*, and I had spent a lunch hour buying the jacket at Alkit. Now Rena was giving me Returned Work because what was good enough for the deputy editor of the *News of the World* wasn't good enough for the plumber. I gave the offending jacket to Laon Maybanks, the photographer, and I may say it is good enough for *him* (bless him). I went back to Alkit and bought another, *very* good leather coat, lined with silk, and Rena was satisfied. She reappeared in England several times that spring, once to buy a small truck (a Mini-Minor, which is, of course, what everyone wants in Greece) and a lot of detergent. As usual I was making lists, and lists of lists, and losing the lists. I had tried, and failed, to get Dunlopillo mattresses delivered somewhere near the island. I had tried, and failed, to get my Moped delivered somewhere near the island. I had tried, and failed, to get the Moped into the back of the car. I had also failed to get the mattresses in. Now Rena cheerfully took on the job of the Moped. I delivered it to her the morning she took delivery of the truck, and away she went, gallantly towing a tiny trailer, filled with detergent and mattresses and Moped.

My sister Liz and I telephoned each other from time to time. We had agreed to meet in Milan. I *think* the reason was that we thought the drive through Italy together would be fun, and I had been told that the Adriatic coast was pretty. Over the telephone, with the Italian Michelin spread on the desk before me, we picked an hotel where we would stay in case of emergency. It was called the Diana Palace (or something like that) and it had a garden, where my sister Liz said she wouldn't mind sitting calmly among the flowers if I didn't turn up. To me it just looked as if it were on a tram track. Oh well, I thought, what the hell. It's only for a night anyway.

I was to leave England about five days before my sister Liz. I was to drive through France (a journey which I always greatly enjoy) in my beautiful convertible Hill-man Superminx. Presently it returned from Rootes, with the back seats out, and chains put in. These were to hold down and lock in the goods that I intended for the house. It poured with rain. In the hall lay my sister's bathing bag, with her flippers for swimming. Poor darling sister Liz. I realised that she was doing her best to get her luggage down to the minimum.

The morning of my departure I got up at 5 a.m. to pack the car. I had a little kitchen table with a Formica top from Woolworth's in cardboard packages. I had two tiny kitchen chairs. Much detergent. Coffee. Food. A tiny methylated-spirit stove in case I didn't get the Calor-gas stove fixed up in my kitchen while I was there. Brushes. Mops. Vim. Ajax, the foaming cleanser. Buckets. Cakes of household soap. Seeds for the garden. A trowel set for gardening *with* . . .

It actually wasn't raining as I loaded my unwieldy cargo. I covered it with the groundsheet, lashed it all down with the chains and left the hood open to the sweet morning air. I actually took the lack of rain for a good omen.

I must have been insane.

EVEN A STRAND OF SPAGHETTI WINDS SOMEWHERE TO THE SEA

For when I turned north, up through Italy from Genoa, it was still raining. It had rained solidly, more than solidly, and the new autostrada from the coast up the mountains was about three feet deep. I had arrived with twenty-four hours to spare, so that sister Liz, getting ready to leave London, should be reassured by a cable with a Milan date-line. This underlines, more than anything else could, the harmless differences in temperament consequent upon our chosen callings.

Sister Liz likes everything cut and dried on holiday, booked down to the last hotel room, and the last five minutes of time. Because all my working life is spent catching deadlines I prefer on holiday to drift and dream, leaving everything to the spur of the moment, trusting to luck, love and the gods. I prefer (indeed I am uncomfortable any other way) to live in a suitcase. She likes all her possessions spread neatly out all around her, particularly on the dressing-table.

So there was I, next day, waiting at the airport. And there eventually was she, looking very pretty indeed, and rather apprehensive, with very little luggage. We stowed it all, without problems of any kind. Indeed, we went spanking back on the autostrada out of Milan again, and all the way to our first hotel with so little incident that I would describe the journey as dull. And the Adriatic coast was dull, too. A big disappointment to me. It came to us through a veil of advertisements for Agip Oil and petrol, and even through a forest of dwarfs, gnomes, replica Davids and Apollos and Venuses. And the Adriatic was grey, slate-grey as the English Channel or the North Sea, and just as uninviting.

Here, too, is another harmless difference in temperament between driver and passenger. When I get a steering wheel between my hands, particularly when the route is rather dull, I find I have to go, go, go, and so my unfortunate sister was whirled from Rimini to Pesaro, from Ancona to Foggia, from Barletta to Bari, and finally to Brindisi. And we were left with a whole day on our hands as a result of my go, go, go, before our ferry sailed from Brindisi to Patras. We enlivened our wait by visiting a weird, decadent-looking place, burnt umber in tone, baroque splendour in shape, with statues and columns and porticos. It was called Lecci, and it lay silent under the Italian sun. Not even a pigeon's coo disturbed the stillness. A clock in the town suddenly chimed a quarter and it made the stillness even more so. In spite of Lecci we both wished there had been some other way of traversing Italy. And when I returned (alone!) I did it even faster, via Foggia, Bovino, Avellino, Naples, Rome and Florence in two glorious days. The road unrolled behind me, the mountains seemed to surge and move under the car. The sun was hot between my shoulder blades, and the wind burnt my face as red as a brick. It would not have done for sister Liz. And even as I revelled in this other journey, stopping only for beer and a sandwich, I knew that my behaviour was hardly civilised.

But the Brindisi–Patras ferry was very civilised indeed.

We were booked into the Italian ship, with a deluxe double cabin and bath for £17 17s. each. Dinner was served in an air-conditioned dining-room all pale mauve and pale yellow, and after dinner I inspected the round swimming-pool, the bar and the sit-up Pullman seats (£5 5s.) so popular and so cheap that they are booked *en bloc* for months ahead, mainly by clubs.

The most famous club in Europe, the Club Mediterranée, which has an enormous membership and travels around in droves in search of sun and sea and good comradeship, regularly books the entire tourist Pullman class on these ferry boats. Mainly they travel around by train, in huge herds, women in beehive hair-dos, neat as only Frenchwomen can be neat, perfectly groomed and brushed, with elegant trousers and impeccable shoes, even at five in the morning. At twelve noon, too, the five hundred members act as one, swigging a dry martini together, and leaping in and out of the pool like well-dressed fish. The Club Mediterranée, organised by cheer leaders, were called to lunch at different times and provided me with an endless display of interest.

The crossing took about twenty-four hours. The boat flirted round Corfu (where it was raining), passed the island of Paxos where my friend Peter Bull has bought land and is building a house, and around six or seven in the evening drew in to Patras.

All the way we had been made aware of Rena's comet-like progress ahead of us. We kept getting cables, saying that the Moped had been held by the Customs at Patras, something to do with the Customs papers. When we arrived at Patras I enquired, vaguely, for it. Yes, it was there and I could take it myself, or give a letter of authority to someone else to take it out for me. For one mad moment I toyed with the idea of lashing it to the outside of the car with rope. But I didn't think that would do, as sister Liz had booked us into A and A.A. hotels all over Greece and it wouldn't look too good, driving up to them. In another even wilder moment I thought I would put the hood down and balance it on top of the household goods. That wouldn't look too good. Then I thought I would try and ride it myself, across the Peloponnese, while sister Liz rested up at a nice hotel. And obviously I abandoned all these schemes as highly impracticable. Later . . . I thought I would try and deal with all that . . . Later.

And so we drove on to Xylokastron, where we were booked to stay the night.

This drive, along the south coast of the Gulf of Corinth, didn't alarm me at all. But then, of course, in a British car the driver is on the *inside* of the road. Poor sister Liz found it hair-raising indeed, all that Greek traffic rushing *at* her. Also, occasionally men waved at us, and this alarmed her. And once I passed a car, of whose rear view I had become tired, and then the car passed us again, furious, and exhibited its disgust by wiggling around all over the road in front of us. All of which upset her very much. By the time we got to Xylokastron she went straight to bed, exhausted, and I picked up a Dutchman in the bar, who turned out to be a Fine Art publisher and editor. It had apparently been pouring with rain for days and my Dutch companion was soaked to the skin. Later, when I crept up to bed, I was very, very sick. So possibly the drive had affected me more than I knew, or I had got altogether too Greek too quickly. Or something.

Next day we went on to Naflion (our next booking) at a sober pace indeed, stopping off en route at Mykinai in the heat of the day to see the palace. I was fresh from Irene Papas's performance as Elektra, and full of the whole story. I was terribly over-excited by the postern gate and the bath and the tomb, and the barren hills and the brooding landscape that must have driven the whole Elektra family dotty, much as the mountains of Norway must have affected Hedda Gabler.

At Naflion, had we heeded it, we had the first mild intimation of the fact that as a pair we might well be allergic to islands. Here we had been booked into an hotel consisting of a converted monastery on a picturesque, rocky islet, far out on the Bay of Argolikos.

'I can't bear it,' I said. 'I can't bear to leave my lovely car here full of household goods on the mainland.'

Sister Liz agreed. And with great dexterity she booked us into another hotel on the mainland, and here we rested up before we moved on to catch the Atlanti-Arkitsa-Aedipsos ferry. Before we made contact with our caique at Orei.

In twelve short months the road to Atlanti was changed indeed. A huge arterial highway stretched, shining, blue-black and good, smack across the Attic Plain, avoiding Levadia, avoiding Thebes.

At Arkitsa now there was quite a big restaurant where there had once been a tiny shack, and there were gorged tourists sitting waiting for the ferry boat amongst the remains of a huge meal. There were even sailors guarding the port, in white ducks, handsome as Errol Flynn. By now sister Liz was nervous again: of being seasick this time. And she leant from the car, gripping her little dictionary, and asked 'Errol' if the sea was going to be rough? He was nonplussed.

All around us, also waiting for the ferry, were about ten single-decker buses, filled to overflowing with beautiful young schoolgirls, Lolitas. They *were* beautiful, these Lolitas, with marvellous antique faces, heavy brows, wonderful eyes: Irene Papases in embryo. They were twittering like starlings amongst themselves. One of them, evidently a senior, detached herself from the group, and came over to the car. 'Can I help you, please?' she asked. She spoke perfect English.

Soon my sister Liz was the centre of a jabbering, admiring and extravagantly fascinated group, all wildly talking English. Soon they disappeared on to the upper deck of the ferry together.

After I had had a beer in the bar I heard wild singing coming from aloft. I climbed the companionway and there they were, my sister Liz and 300 Greek schoolgirls, singing away like thrushes in the hot afternoon sun. They sang 'Arividerci Roma' and 'Romantica' and the *Never on Sunday* tune. And then they suddenly called out 'Tweest!' A girl dashed down to the bus and came back with a battery-operated pick-up. Someone put on Chubby Checker in the Peppermint Lounge. 'Let's Twist Again . . . Like we did last Summer!' rang out across the Channel of Euboia. And my sister (who twists extremely well) was soon the centre of a delighted twisting throng. By and by, a man in blue jeans and a faded blue shirt, gold religious medals bouncing on his sunburnt throat, pushed through the crowd and took over my sister, twisting like a mad thing. The ship ploughed steadily through a sea like blue satin. The captain and the man at the wheel could scarcely be seen for the schoolgirls' faces. They surrounded the wheelhouse, the upper deck, the superstructure, like flowers in a film star's cabin.

'Who on earth is *he*?' cried my sister as she noticed the man in jeans, and he let out a few rhythmic hoots in time to his own twisting.

'He is the bus-driver!' cried the girls.

I doubt if the Euboia Channel, even in ancient times, when Euboia was supposed to be the home of the centaurs, ever witnessed a more astonishing, or more charming, scene.

Chapter Eight

The Water Man Cometh

At Orei the caique was waiting. We loaded the car on without incident. The voyage, under the sun, which was cooking up nicely now, passed without event. We tried to talk to the caique men. The thing was hopeless. For some reason there was no question of communication. Unlike every other Greek I have ever met they simply didn't want to talk. I gave up. Lulled half asleep by the slopping of the sea against the caique's flanks, equally lulled by the plop, plop, plop of the engine's exhaust, I dreamed the afternoon away. By and by Skiathos swam up out of the heat haze. By and by I pulled myself together and made other efforts to communicate. I started to try and identify my own little white box of a house amongst the other little white boxes dotted here and there on the green headlands. In one year there seemed to have been a hell of a lot of houses built, standing out white and bright against the green of the scrub and the gold of the sand. After about my eleventh cry of wolf! wolf! and my house! my house! I collapsed into a sulky silence, peering, peering at the coastline of perpetual, interminable charm . . .

247

Eventually, slopping, slapping, we came thudding into the harbour at Skiathos. There was Gus Merodes again. No difficulty in communicating with him, thank goodness. Same warm, dry hand clasp. Same gleaming, reassuring steel-rimmed glasses, same efficiency in getting cars off caiques. Under Gus's supervision the car was off the caique in a flash. Now, what were we to do? Where were we booked? At which unlikely hostelry along the water-front would we try first . . .

As I was about to start banging on doors, through the silent crowd, who were already fed up with us as a mid-afternoon spectacle, there came the violence of a powerful motor-bike, driven at speed. Mounted on it, very dashing, a man of medium height with (I think) a small soft moustache. He was wearing a leather jacket. On the pillion behind him, a handsome youth in shirt-sleeves. The pair of them came to a spectacular halt and the youth said something in Greek to Gus.

Gus turned to me apologetically.

'Mrs Rena she says you go to her house. Follow the man on the motor-bike. He show the way. Remember, it is difficult to get out of the village.'

True enough. I remembered. Gus and I said good-bye. Then we clambered into the car and followed the motor-bike, through the crazy streets, wiggling in and out of mules and donkeys and old ladies as before, past landmarks that I had begun at last to identify from all my other island adventures. There was the fountain, for example, with its slowly running, sparkling cold

Kala Nero (Good Water). The water comes all the way down from the mountains and as it springs out in the street it is surrounded by women, boys of all ages, children, toddlers. Round the corner we came, dusty and noisy, and all the little urchins of Skiathos, snotty-nosed, dirty-kneed, came galloping after us, all of them barefooted, all of them springing in the air and shouting.

The motor-bike twirled ahead of us, busy as a cock-chafer on a pin. We rushed past the army camp, where the same Greek gods were still standing at ease. We dashed along the coast. The sea lay below us, blue and green as ever, and there suddenly on the road ahead of us was Rena. In my recollections of her Rena is always wearing a bikini, and it took several seconds before I recognised this distinguished, elegant lady in a white embroidered blouse and sincere skirt, walking along the cliff-top, accompanied by a dog. She was the very picture of the aristocratic land-owner taking an evening stroll through her demesne.

Greetings. Explanations. Of course we were staying with her. Absolute nonsense. No trouble at all. And also, of *course*, we wanted to see the house at once.

'He will take you there on his motor-bike,' said Rena. 'Actually, he is the plumber.' And she laughed.

Of course. I might have recognised the leather jacket. I wanted to know about it. Had he liked it? Was it at last good enough? And on top of that how about the drains? Were they working? Were they good enough? Could

I try them? I wanted to know a thousand things now, immediately, at once . . .

Staring back at us, across the bay, precisely as we had planned it, was the little blank face of the house, staring down into the lapis sea like a white kitten. That in itself was miracle enough. Was I asking too much of it to have drains and a water closet as well?

Sister Liz, very intrepid, clambered on the pillion of the motor-bike and clasped the plumber round the middle. They roared off together round the headland. Yes, along the General's Road. It really was complete then. It really did lead right up to my door.

Rena and I gazed after their cloud of dust. It hung behind them in the air like one of those 'Thinks' balloons in the comic strip. Rena introduced me to a perfectly splendid lady in a pink cotton dress called Teresa. (I confused matters no end by referring to her constantly, and always as *Tesera*, which is the Greek for the figure 4.) I wandered through Rena's house and out on to her patio. This being whitewashed threw back an agonising glare. But it was civilisation personified. On it stood seats, swing garden hammocks, low tables, sofas. I goggled at the hard work Rena had put in, fetching furniture from the mainland. I thought of the cost of caiques, loaded down to the gunwales. I thought of beds, mattresses . . . As I pondered everything she had achieved I became deeply disappointed in myself.

The plumber came roaring back on his bike.

Now it was my turn to cling to him. Away we went,

at a brisk thirty miles an hour, swooping and swerving in and out the red-clay embankments, cracking here and there in the sun, of the General's Road. It had apparently rained so much during the winter in the meadows in the valley below our two houses, where James Jones's house may presently be, that the marshy bottom was ever so slightly flooded. The bike went through what amounted to a morass with an emphatic splash and swish. Then we climbed a gradient roughly one in five and I was suddenly there.

There was the little white house, exactly as I had dreamed it. There was the front door, the little porch, the olive tree growing up, precisely as it had been planned.

Sister Liz was standing in the doorway, all beaming smiles.

'It's perfectly beautiful,' she said. 'Perfectly beautiful. Far, far better than I had imagined.'

And the plumber ran through the house eager to demonstrate his taps and his water closet.

He couldn't. There was no water in the tank. Crest-fallen, he went back to his motor-bike.

Next day the water man came, gaunt-necked like a turtle, wearing one of those battered flat hats with straws sticking out of it. He agreed to fill the tank so that the w.c. might flush. It then appeared that Rena's tank hadn't been filled for some weeks either, and *her* w.c. wouldn't flush. Like the title of an unwritten play by O'Neill we arranged for the water man to come and fill the tanks for about fifteen shillings.

And when we had arranged to have the tank full, and adequate water for washing, Rena organised a working party of Tesera (sorry, there I go again, Teresa) and the boy who had ridden pillion on the bike (she explained him as a messenger able to speak English) to scrub through the floors and remove the filth left by the workmen.

'Oh, and to pick up the sacks and things left by the workmen and burn them,' added sister Liz brightly. 'Else there will shortly be flies.'

Next day the water man cometh. And I made the interesting discovery that there was no staircase up to the roof. Every gallon of water (and the tank holds a hell of a lot) had to be carried, in five-gallon drums, up a slant of about forty-five degrees on a plank six inches wide, ten feet up. The mule stopped. The water man put down five five-gallon drums, many of them without stoppers, bunches of fern and peppermint holding the water loosely in its place.

There was no need for words to know what the expression meant on the water man's face. It meant, '*I'm* not going up that bloody plank, no *sir* . . .'

I DREAMT I HAD DRAINS IN MY MAIDEN-FORM BRA . . .

Maddened, I rushed up the plank myself, closely followed by Tesera. We were both determined to prove to the men how hopeless they were. The men weren't so stupid. They stood on the ground and let Tesera and me fill the tank alone. (Tesera was a delightful character.

She wore one cotton dress, even sleeping in it, curled up in Rena's living-room, like a lovable pet. She was very strong and felt melancholy when she wasn't working, but she didn't really understand electricity and things like that. There was a terrible episode when she took Rena's iron and heated it up on the Calor-gas cooker to press a skirt and so ruined the element.)

Next day I faced the plumber across a table in Rena's living-room and counted out to him travellers' cheques to the value of about £100. This represented fees carefully saved as a result of my first little lecture tour in America. We had already eaten together and I had become quite fond of the plumber as a personality. But the £100 I counted out represented lectures in Fall River, Massachusetts, a girls' school in Gadsden, a morning of near prayer in Bethlehem, Pennsylvania, and at least one Town Hall in Michigan where I had yacked at the ladies for an hour at 10.15 a.m. from the stage of a huge cinema.

The £100 represented at least five thousand miles of travel, by Trailways bus, by Peter Pan bus, by tiny aeroplanes like moths (where they feed you on chewing gum and chocolate), hopping from Alabama to the Milwaukee English Speaking Group. They represented so many hours in loneliness, sweat, tension and stage-fright.

As I counted them out, I couldn't help thinking it was extremely odd that these hours had now been converted into a bath, a w.c., a sink and a bathroom basin.

I wondered which of us, in our several ways, worked the harder.

Then Rena and the plumber went off to Volos. I prepared to go across and scrub my little house through.

Tesera was a terrific worker. She stood there, pushing a sort of pan scrubber along the tiles with her foot. I joined in, with many shouts of '*Bravo!*' (Good). I unloaded the two camp-beds from the car and set them up in the study and in the master bedroom. I set out the kitchen table with the blue Formica top under my study window, and put a little kitchen chair on either side of it. It was like a monk's tiny pale blue cell with a beige floor, except that no monk in all the world ever had a view like that from his cell. As I twirled the butterfly nuts to assemble the table-top I felt rather clever.

Sister Liz lay down on one of the camp-beds and brooded. I don't blame her. The world is divided into designers, scrubbers and assemblers of Woolworth tables. I am a scrubber, that's all. There is nothing drearier for a designer than a scrubber in action.

'*Why* can't you let *them* do that?' said my sister Liz.

Next day the water man left only ten gallons of water and made not the slightest effort to trot up the plank and pour them into the tank. He also refused to clear up the workmen's refuse. He said it would start a forest fire. I then discovered a fascinating fact about myself. *I* don't care to run up a plank and risk a broken leg *unless* there is someone watching. Still, I had enough water in the tank for a good flush. And flush I did. I well and truly declared the drains of my little house open. But it did cross my mind once or twice that if I had had an architect supervising the job originally, the chances are that he would not have forgotten the staircase up to the roof and the tank.

Then, just as I was hoping for peace and quietness, so that I could brood in my monk's cell, I noticed a rowing boat putting in at the big curving beach below the house. A heavy, laden rowing boat, with what appeared to be a cupboard insecurely balanced on it.

The carpenters. There were two of them. Quite jolly men, wearing black Basque berets. Cheerfully whistling between their teeth they started crashing nails into the woodwork as they assembled some loose cupboard-shaped arrangements of beaver-board and three-ply and pitch-pine framework. Watching them, encouraging them with occasional moans of '*Bravo . . . bravo*', it passed through my mind that Rutterford and I could have done all that, *and* had fun, for half the cost, in half the time and without any fuss at all.

In the heat of the day everyone knocked off and sister Liz and I stopped trying to communicate with the carpenters. She was gripping her little dictionary, explaining that a thing that was allegedly a dressing-table (of extreme horror) just wouldn't *do*. I suggested to her we should go swimming, on Alfred Allan's and my old beach. 'I know it's nice,' I said with enthusiasm. 'I know it's perfectly lovely.'

So we got our bathing dresses and we reversed the car on to the road and we went along to the Garden of Eden.

There were *people* there.

I don't mean Pa, Ma and the baby. Obviously they were there. They were very sweet, and they hugged me and asked Where was Kyrius, and they were thrilled to meet The Sister. They were sitting under a tree in the sun.

No, the people were a German water-diviner and an Englishman who had hired him to divine water so that he might dig a well. *He* had bought one of the headlands overlooking Pa and Ma and the baby's beach. He was just starting on *his* headaches.

We changed. We swam. Or did we even? I scarcely remember. For almost immediately the water-diviner called out that *eine grosse Fische* had eaten a lady there only yesterday. Sister Liz and I were furious. We whirled through her little dictionary, came up with some good Greek words for 'wild savage fish'. And we plunged at Ma asking her if the water-diviner was telling the truth.

Ma shook her head. She had clearly never heard of such nonsense in her life. But the water-diviner, obviously hell-bent on spoiling our afternoon, waved his hands about and continued to give a disastrous imitation of *eine grosse Fische* eating a lady.

'What a horrible man,' said sister Liz. 'It's all rot, of course. He simply wants us off this beach . . . But beaches are public property. They belong to the Queen in England, so I bet they belong to the King here.'

'Well, it's certainly put me off,' I said, sadly.

Wistfully I looked across the blue-green water about

which I had once been so possessive. We tried another beach. There was *jam* on that. Jam, with a huge procession of ants carrying it about from here to there. Jam on the beach. Men pretending there were grosse fisches. And all in twelve short months. And the happy atmosphere of the place was all gone, too. Everywhere one went there were little groups of scowling faces, arguing about wells, and employing expensive men with twigs. And there were people down in the port who one short year ago had been children of nature, to whom the 'stranger was sacred'.

In twelve months the sacred stranger had become the not-so-sacred tourist.

Chapter Nine

The Shadow of Mount Athos

I recognised with some clarity that the island adventure was over, anyway for that year. Rena had done her best. The plumber had done his best. The water man had not been very co-operative, but there, it can't be much fun being a water man, anyway. Sister Liz and I had done our best. But in all sobriety, if the object of the exercise was a healing holiday for the nerves, nobody could be expected to hang around, chatting up the carpenters with a little dictionary, arguing all day long about the price of this and the workmanship of that. And there wasn't even a light-hearted pretence at privacy. Even the beaches were as dirty as Southend, Margate or Brighton on August Bank Holiday.

That night was the night of the full moon. Incredible touching beauty, serenely sailing over the troubled island, releasing tears in my heart and in my sister's heart as well. But having made the decision that it was useless to linger I thought we had best remove ourselves.

I drove down to the port and found Gus. I ordered the caique for the next morning. I had conversations with a builder and told him I needed a staircase out-side my house, so I could put water in my tank, and a staircase down into the sea at the deep point. To avoid the beach. I shook hands with everyone, and as I drove back to the house there was that curious throbbing in the air peculiar to primitive islands. I didn't sleep at all that night.

When the caique sailed next day I began to feel better. 'I have lost a battle,' I said to myself, 'but I have not lost the war.' My heart was lightening all the way to Orei and by the time we had reached Aedipsos and the ferry I was in very good form. We decided to go to Loutraki, which Dilys Powell had mentioned in her book *An Affair of the Heart*, and there we found a very good hotel, a lady who thought we were 'lovelee' and masses of hot bath-water. The beach was clean. The people who were bathing from it were quiet and well-behaved. It was very difficult to discuss Skiathos.

'It has never been colonised by any of the ancient civilisations,' said my sister, with a great gravity. 'And that makes a difference to a place. I mean, I found it very *witchy*. All those bundles of hyssop hanging over the doors and the full moon and everything. It says here in this book that there are witches in Thessaly who "call down the moon" which causes lameness and blindness, and if you look at the map Skiathos is just a little bit of Thessaly broken off into the sea.'

'Skiathos means the shadow of Mount Athos,' I said. 'It's always worried me that it is nowhere near Mount

Athos and the shadow of Mount Athos falls nowhere near it whatsoever . . .'

'Athos is the place where the Apollonian worship of good sense and reason was carried on,' said sister Liz.

'Mmm,' I said.

'So I suppose Skiathos could mean the dark side of the sun.'

Fanciful indeed. Rubbish, I thought to myself. But somehow I thought it best not to mention too often that Roy Rutterford and his temperamental friend had *both* broken their legs after their trip to the island.

I have met a witch or two in my time and they always seem to me infinitely pathetic with all that voodoo and idiocy and carry-on.

So we drove to the resort of Loutraki, where the ever-freshening winds from the Gulf of Corinth restored us to sanity. We bathed a great deal. Then I drove sister Liz into Athens and she flew away to join her husband in the South of France.

As for me, I bought a newspaper or two and drove slowly into the Piraeus to find my ferry boat. Before I left England I had booked on a vessel that was billed to sail all the way from Piraeus to Brindisi via Patras. It would save me the long hot dusty journey along the coast road via Xylokastron.

Eventually, in the hot, bright, gritty streets of the Piraeus I found an English-speaking young lady in the company offices. She deeply regretted that the boat wouldn't sail. It was still in dry dock. I regretted it, too.

What did she suggest? She shrugged, in the inimitable Greek manner. I could drive to Patras, as one or other of the ferry boats, Italian or Greek, *always* left Patras for Brindisi every evening. To her horror I burst out laughing. I bowed goodbye. I went back to the car. There on the outside of all the newspapers was the headline announcing Profumo's resignation. There was the announcement of Stephen Ward's arrest. I knew darned well that I should go back to England, at once, at once, and not linger there, over the cold ashes of my love affair with the landscape of Greece. Could I telephone? No, I could not, there was a strike. Could I cable? Tomorrow I would be able to cable. Damn and hell and blast, I thought. I'll get back to Italy and telephone from there . . .

I began, for the second time that day, the drive along the Gulf of Corinth. It was very hot. It became hotter and hotter. Soon I couldn't stand it another second. Risky it might be, all alone on that highway, on that road constantly whirling with the dust of trucks and buses and lorries, but I *had* to swim in that sea.

In extreme discomfort I changed in the car, crouched over the steering wheel. I locked the car with care, and with the key in my teeth I hurdled over the shingle to sand and warm, warm rocks. There were tiny crisp waves in the gulf, wind-blown waves, quite big enough for breakers. Here, in the toe of my sandals I left my car key. And I slid into that unbelievably beautiful sea. As usual, Poseidon worked his magic for me. All my primitive anger, all my nerves and annoyance at my return to my real world floated away from me in the Gulf of Corinth.

Floating there, rising and falling slightly to the waves, turning my face up to the sun, towards Apollo, I remembered my last flight from the island, with Alfred Allan Lewis up to Delphi.

IT TAKES AN ORACLE TO KNOW WHEN

Then we had travelled so slowly up to Delphi, so slowly. And halfway up the mountain from the plain we were held up for a good twenty minutes while some men quarried stone with high explosive. We had ample opportunity to take it all in, the barren hillside, the herds of goats, black goats with yellow eyes and slobbering tongues. They looked in league with the devil there, and the shepherds didn't look exactly from the Good Book, strolling along the mountainside in their shapeless blankets and battered hats.

As we rose it became colder and colder. The clouds were descending, shrouding the upper slopes in thick white mists. After our excesses of sun and sand and sea it was a relief indeed.

Eventually the single street of Delphi appeared.

'Look,' I said to Alfred Allan. 'I have had a "thing" about the Charioteer all my life, ever since I saw him in Arthur Mee's *1,000 Beautiful Things* when I was at school. May I go and see him before the museum closes?'

'Aw right,' said Alfred Allan. 'Aw right.'

I found a parking space outside the museum. I fled up the stairs. And there I encountered the charming, vacant, infinitely stupid gaze of the brown-eyed Charioteer. Dusk was creeping round the museum. Hadrian's Antinous, charming but a bit fat, stood in the same room. I smiled, remembering my sister's remarks about him: 'A good reliable, steadfast lad. Would make an excellent footman.' So he had, made an excellent footman, Antinous. So he had . . .

And then the guards came to tell us that the museum was closing and we had to turn away.

'Never mind,' said Alfred Allan. 'We'll still be here tomorrow and you can come and see them both again.'

Was it the contrast, that I had come to Delphi straight from such desperations of un-plumbing, and the plumbing in the new Delphi hotel is of such superiority and quality? Or was it the water itself, endlessly flowing, purifying me from the Catalan Spring? Alfred Allan and I *wallowed* in our bathrooms, occasionally stepping out on to our balconies to compare notes, gazing down the valley, over endless grey-green olive trees that seemed to be foaming down to the sea. We did not stir out of our bathrooms for four whole hours when we arrived in Delphi. And then, by common consent, we changed into evening dress and drank dry martinis, shaken up by the barman in the hotel bar.

Oh, civilisation. Oh, dry martini. Oh, ice in the drinks. Oh, plumbing.

★

There was more to civilisation than these things, I reflected as I stood in Delphi a year later, after sister Liz had left. Guidebook in hand I walked the Sacred Way to the temples of Apollo and his sister Athena: with the sun warm on my shoulders I stood in the market place where, thousands of years ago, people like myself had wondered what to ask the Oracle.

All around me crickets ticked. The peace of Delphi washed over me, in endless waves of sight and sound and smell and sensation.

In the amphitheatre I felt it most. Here on one of the stone seats I sat and listened lazily to guides from different countries. I watched a crippled lady, her legs in irons, smile with pleasure and gratitude. I watched a school of blind children, taking in through their ears the beauty they could not see.

I closed *my* eyes. I felt the butterflies zig-zag by. A pigeon cooed somewhere, throatily. A labouring motor engine coughed on the road. Here in the cool sunlight was the healing atmosphere that has made Delphi one of the shrines of the world.

At peace, unworried, unhurried, I clambered down. I stood on the spot where since time immemorial people have laid bare their hearts to the Oracle, asking for guidance.

I did not speak my thoughts aloud. Somewhere far inside my mind, silently as a worm in coral, I framed the question: 'Please, dear Apollo, tell me what sort of book I should write?'

I opened my eyes again.

A British tourist was on her way towards me, unmistakably to ask for an autograph. I shut my eyes.

'Miss Spain?' she asked. 'Is it?'

I nodded, dumbly.

'Well,' she said, cheerfully, 'I wish you would write us another book like *Thank You, Nelson*. True, you know, and funny, of course, but how you feel about things.'

And she wandered away, leaving me speechless on the slopes of Parnassus. I expected 'service', of course, from the Oracle. But not *such* service, and so quickly. Apollo's messenger, wearing a shapeless raincoat and carrying a sketch-book. Fancy that.

And if all our twentieth century should be swept away, I thought, following her down, rock by rock; when the grass grows in Wall Street, and the vines have split the pavements of Piccadilly, and the fig trees are heavy with fruit where Paris once stood – I wonder what the archaeologists will make of us?

Everything in my personal struggle suddenly seemed so small and childish, my little rebellions seemed so little worthwhile beside the beautifully planned, carefully spontaneous columns of Delphi. Since the beginning, madam, I thought, almost ready to call it after her, man has paused at Delphi to offer himself up to reason and to clarity. Praying, as I do now, to accept the truth about myself.

Wherever you are, madam, with your sketch-book and your battered mac, here is the book you asked me to write.

Appendix

(see page 225)
The author's account of the Doxiadis report is, in fact, a fairly light-hearted résumé. For the readers who are interested in the details, Sir Basil Spence's letter to the celebrated architect, and the résumé which Dr Doxiadis made of the local architect's report to him, appear below by kind permission of Sir Basil and Dr Doxiadis.

Dr Constantinos Doxiadis,
Technological Institute,
Athens, Greece.

My dear Doxiadis,

Can I prevail on our acquaintanceship for some help and I know that this is asking a steam hammer to crack a pistachio nut.

When you were in England you may have heard of Nancy Spain who is one of our most celebrated writers, a very distinguished journalist and broadcaster and is really a famous person. She visited Greece and fell in love with the country (who hasn't!!) and she bought a site on the island of Skiathos and embarked on the hazardous venture of building a house there. The arrangements appear to have been friendly and casual and several things are worrying her very deeply, one is, will the house ever have running water and drains and, second, she has paid over a large sum of money to Mrs Rena Harper who is a Greek married to an English man and she is acting as agent. I believe she has given Mrs Harper £1,000 for sending to the builder when he requires money and is due for payment. She does not know the name of the builder but, no doubt, this could be found out on the spot.

My request is simply that you ask one of your assistants to go and visit the site, please find out what is happening and let me know. Nancy Spain is quite willing to meet the expenses and a fee for this. If, on the other hand, this is too small for you and your assistants, please let me know but perhaps you may be able to suggest some other architect who would be willing to render this little service which would be so gratefully acknowledged.

I am enclosing all the maps which Miss Spain has sent me including a large scale one showing the island and the position of her site together with a photostat 'plan' and a photograph of the little house which looks so forlorn.

The memory of your discourse is vivid still as without a doubt the R.I.B.A. has never had such a full house and I

was very proud to be President during this great occasion.
With kindest regards to you and your wife,

> Yours very sincerely,
> signed BASIL SPENCE

REPORT ON THE VISIT TO MISS NANCY SPAIN'S HOUSE
NOW UNDER CONSTRUCTION IN SKIATHOS

1. The contractor and I visited the site where the house of Miss Spain is being built. There I ascertained that the following work has already been carried out:

(a) Construction of exterior and interior walls in accordance with the design.

(b) Concrete roof slab and a small parapet.

(c) Internal and external plastering.

(d) Internal water supply installations, together with sanitary fittings (W.C., lavatory basin, bath) and sink, installed complete. A water tank, on the terrace, is connected with them.

(e) Cesspool which is actually a septic tank because it has been dug into a rocky ground. I found it full of rain water. It is covered by a concrete slab with a manhole. The pipes that will connect the bathroom with the pit have not been placed yet, but the necessary preparation of the ground has been made.

(f) Windows and doors, exterior and interior, with their handles but without any finishing (priming, etc.).

(g) Concrete floor.

2. Although I was not in a position to make detailed measurement and calculations, I can say that the value of work carried out so far has certainly exceeded the sum of about £1,000 that Miss Spain has made available, in view of the fact that all the materials have to be transported from a distance and not with means that would necessarily qualify as modern means of transport.

3. Local conditions in general should be taken into account in evaluating the quality of the work. With this in view the construction can be considered as good except for the internal doors and windows which have warped and do not shut well. There is also an objection as to the concrete mix, in which aggregates from the sea have been used (sand, gravel) without being at least splashed. The contractor told me that in order to counterbalance this disadvantage they pour more cement and that this is the system followed in all the constructions of the island.

4. Another remark concerns the cess-pit. The drains of the kitchen and the bathroom should empty into the same cess-pit and not into two different ones as it is intended. I was not able to ascertain the depth of the pit because it was full of rain water, as I mentioned already. However, holes can be bored leading to a less hard layer so as to increase the absorbing capacity of the pit.

5. In the continuation of the work, top priority must be given to the repair and painting of the doors and windows. Then a few minor repairs of the plastering have to be made because the piping of the plumbing was made after plastering, the veranda must be constructed and the

kitchen and bathroom must be connected with the pit. Finally a decision should be taken as to the water supply.

6. The question of water is a matter of expenditure and luck. There are indications that water exists in the area. However, neither its quantity and quality nor the depth at which water can be found are known. The cost will be around £200–£400 because in addition to the excavation and construction of a well, a hand operated or mechanically driven pump and piping will be required in order to pump the water into the tank on the terrace from where it will be distributed to the house. In case water is not found it can be bought from the villagers who transport it with pack animals in summertime, or rain water can be collected on the terrace of the house, stored in a water tank and pumped into the terrace tank. This system is followed in all the Aegean islands wherever water is scarce. Chlorination can also be effected, to ensure sterilisation.

signed K. KATSOUFIS, Architect

Help us make the next generation of readers

We – both author and publisher – hope you enjoyed this book. We believe that you can become a reader at any time in your life, but we'd love your help to give the next generation a head start.

Did you know that 9% of children don't have a book of their own in their home, rising to 13% in disadvantaged families*? We'd like to try to change that by asking you to consider the role you could play in helping to build readers of the future.

We'd love you to think of sharing, borrowing, reading, buying or talking about a book with a child in your life and spreading the love of reading. We want to make sure the next generation continue to have access to books, wherever they come from.

And if you would like to consider donating to charities that help fund literacy projects, find out more at **www.literacytrust.org.uk** and **www.booktrust.org.uk**.

THANK YOU

*As reported by the National Literacy Trust